Veronika Müller

Salads

VNR VAN NOSTRAND REINHOLD
_____New York

CONTENTS

Preface

Salads have for long been considered merely a simple part of our food intake, but in recent years have established a stronger position in our daily diet. Today's professional chef has progressed a long way from the tired green salads which were all too often seen in hotel and restaurant dining rooms of the past. People have become far more health conscious and discriminating, and whether in their homes or when eating out at restaurants, are looking for a variety and a choice in salads. Because the salad is more than a simple accompaniment, and can often be considered as a main dish of high value in its own right, the reader will find sections in this book devoted to the more substantial salad.

Salads have always been an important part of traditional European and American cookery, and more recently in Nouvelle Cuisine. This book contains many recipes for traditional well known salads, together with a great number of imaginative dishes which are both appetising and easy to prepare.

In addition, there are exciting recipes for light, healthy fruit salads as desserts, and also for unusual salads which combine both fruits and vegetables.

The superb colour photographs throughout this book will give the reader countless ideas, and will guide the professional to better presentation.

In today's climate of healthy eating, when more and more people are rightly concerned with the nutritional value of what they eat, this exciting new book will fill a gap on many kitchen bookshelves.

8

Fresh Salads in Season

We eat salads because we enjoy their freshness and crisp flavour and to help us achieve a well balanced diet. They complement fish, meat, game and egg-dishes when served as a side dish.

The Lettuce family

Lettuce, also known as green salad is the best-known of the five various members of the garden salad.

Batavia is a new type of lettuce developed in France, the leaves of which go from green to a brown colour towards the tip. The same items and sauces go with it as with lettuce.

More sensitive treatment is necessary with oak-leaf lettuce in order that its nutty flavour is not overwhelmed. It is also a newcomer from France, whose wild origins stem from North Africa. Oak-leaf lettuce is dark with strongly-feathered leaves which wilt very quickly.

Lettuce with Grapes

200 grams/7 oz black grapes	
1 fully ripe peach	
100 grams/3½ oz canned satsuma oranges	
1 large lettuce	
3 tablespoons crème fraîche or soured cream	
2 tablespoons juice from the satsumas	
2 tablespoons sherry- or red wine-vinegar	
1 tablespoon walnut- or almond-oil	
salt	
white pepper from the mill	
1 pinch ground coriander	

Wash the grapes and let drain. Pick them from the stalks, and halve them, removing the pips. Blanch the peach in boiling water, and leave it in for 1 minute, before peeling. Halve the peach, remove the stone and chop the flesh into small dice.
Drain off the satsumas.
Clean the lettuce, removing any unwanted leaves, separate the leaves, wash and dry them, then pull them to pieces, removing any hard centre stems.
Beat together the soured cream, satsuma juice, vinegar and oil with a whisk into a frothy sauce. Flavour with salt, pepper, and coriander to a piquant taste.
Mix all the salad ingredients lightly but thoroughly into the sauce and serve immediately. This salad goes well with all light roasts, grills and poached fish fillets.

Preparation time: 20 minutes
Finishing time: 5 minutes

Batavia Salad with Almonds

1 head of batavia lettuce	
3 spring onions	
4 sprigs of basil	
4 large leaves of borage	
40 grams/1½ oz flaked almonds	
5 grams/⅙ oz butter	
3 tablespoons sherry vinegar	
2 tablespoons dry sherry (fino)	
1 pinch herb mustard	
1 tiny pinch sugar	
salt, white pepper from mill	
5 tablespoons cold-pressed olive oil (see p. 54)	

Clean and pull the batavia to pieces. Wash the leaves and spin-dry.
Clean the spring onions, chipping the white part finely and cutting the green into 5 mm/ ¼ inch lengths.
Rinse and dry well the borage and basil.
Pick the basil leaves from the stalks and cut the borage leaves into fine strips.
Lightly fry off the flaked almonds in the butter in a non-stick pan. Dry off on a piece of kitchen tissue.
Mix the sherry vinegar, sherry, mustard and the flavourings into a smooth sauce until the salt and sugar have dissolved, then beat in the olive oil with a balloon whisk until the sauce is light and creamy.
Mix all salad ingredients except the almonds into the sauce.
Sprinkle the salad with the almond flakes and serve immediately.
The salad goes especially well with all sorts of lightly roasted meats, uncoated fried fish fillets, truite au bleu, and venison steaks.

Preparation time: 20 minutes
Finishing time: 5 minutes

Oak Leaf Lettuce in Cream Dressing

1 large or 2 small heads of oak-leaf lettuce

25 grams/1 oz extremely thinly cut smoked salmon

1 bunch dill

1 small glass of crème fraîche or soured cream 100 grams/$3\frac{1}{2}$ oz

4 tablespoons cream

2 tablespoons lemon juice

salt, cayenne pepper, Worcestershire sauce

Pull the oak-leaf lettuce to pieces, wash thoroughly and spin-dry.
Cut the smoked-salmon into extremely thin slices and cut finely.
Rinse off the dill, dab it dry and cut finely.
Beat the soured cream, cream and lemon juice with a balloon whisk into a frothy sauce and season it with salt, cayenne pepper and a little Worcestershire sauce to give a piquant flavour. Mix in the dill.
Divide the salad into four portions and pour over the cream dressing.
Garnish with the smoked salmon.
The salad goes especially well with kidneys, or stewed calf's liver served with a rice border, or with lightly roasted game.

Preparation time: 15 minutes
Finishing time: 5 minutes

Spinach Salad with Bacon

300 grams/11 oz spinach leaves

2 hard-boiled eggs

125 grams/4 oz mild smoked streaky bacon

1 teaspoon sharp mustard

3 tablespoons herb vinegar

white pepper from mill

3 tablespoons cold-pressed olive oil

3 tablespoons red wine vinegar

Look over the spinach leaves. Cut off the stalks, wash the leaves, leave to drain, or spin dry. Shell the eggs, cut into halves and remove the yolks. Press the yolks through a sieve and chop the whites finely. Cut the bacon into small dice and fry off lightly over a low heat in a pan until the fat is crisp. Mix the mustard, egg yolks, herb vinegar and pepper together. Beat strongly with a balloon whisk while gradually adding the olive oil. Take the bacon dice from the pan and discard all but a third of the bacon fat. Mix the spinach in a bowl with the bacon dice and the egg white. Mix the remaining bacon fat with the red-wine vinegar, cook off and pour the mixture over the salad. Serve immediately. Spinach salad goes well with white meats and with rich boiled or fried fish.

Preparation time: 15 minutes. Finishing time: 5 minutes.

Note: This salad tastes best made with tender young summer spinach leaves. If you wish to make it in winter, as the leaves are very thick and somewhat strong in flavour, it is best to blanch them first in boiling water, then drain them and dry them on a layer of kitchen tissue, but a small part of the valuable vitamin C will be lost.

Lamb's Lettuce in Sour Cream

200 grams/7 oz lamb's lettuce

100 grams/3½ oz thinly sliced bacon

2 cloves garlic

2 anchovy fillets

3 tablespoons sherry- or wine-vinegar

3 tablespoons walnut oil

3 tablespoons thick sour cream or crème fraîche

salt, white pepper

1 pinch sugar

1 slice white toasting bread

10 grams/⅓ oz butter

Lamb's lettuce is the most tender of the winter salads, and especially rich in vitamins A and C and contains as much iron as parsley.
Lamb's lettuce is also known as corn salad.
The tender structure of the leaves means that great care must be taken by growers, as strong fertilisers have an adverse effect on the flavour. Remove all roots and any weak plants with yellow leaves, then wash very carefully, at least twice, as lamb's lettuce in general is very sandy.
Drain off the leaves well in a colander.
Lay the bacon slices in a sieve and pour over boiling water.
Let drain off then dab dry with kitchen tissue and cut into thin strips.
Peel one of the cloves of garlic and chop it finely or press through a garlic press.
Rinse off the anchovy fillets, then dab dry and chop finely. Mix them together with the garlic, vinegar, oil and sour cream.
Season with the salt, pepper and sugar.
Peel the second clove of garlic and rub it well over the slice of bread. Cut the bread into small cubes.
Heat the butter in a small pan and lightly fry off the diced bread until browned and crisp. In between times, mix the salad leaves with the sauce and the bacon.
Sprinkle the bread cubes over the salad and serve immediately.

The salad goes especially well with game dishes, steaks and roast beef.

Preparation time: 15 minutes
Finishing time: 10 minutes

12

13

The Chicory Family

Chicory, scarole and curly endive are, like (Belgian) endive and radicchio, newcomers to the chicory scene. While they were once winter salad-stuffs, they now appear in summer as well, and the summer varieties are often less bitter.

Scarole is smooth and broad-leaved, while chicory has smaller crinkled leaves. Curly endive has light, white to yellow frizzy many-pointed leaves.

Chicory Salad with Olives

1 head of chicory

1 bunch of radishes

4 spring onions

1 box mustard and cress

50 grams/2 oz green olives stuffed with red peppers

1 tablespoon capers

1 egg yolk

1 teaspoon mustard

1 pinch sugar

salt, white pepper

3 tablespoons wine vinegar

4 tablespoons cold-pressed olive oil

2 tablespoons cream

Clean up the chicory, then cut off the bottom so that the leaves separate.
Wash the leaves, spin-dry and cut diagonally into 3 cm/ 1¼ inch strips.
Clean the radishes, wash and dry them, then cut them into thin slices.

Clean the spring onions. Wash and dry them, chopping the white part finely, and cutting the green across into short lengths.
Wash the cress, spin it dry, then cut off the leaves.
Halve the drained olives. Chop the capers roughly.
Press the egg-yolk through a sieve, add the mustard, sugar, salt and pepper, mixing all together with the wine vinegar. Beat in the oil, then finally the cream. Mix all the salad ingredients together with the sauce in a large bowl, leave to stand for 5 minutes, then dress into a serving dish, and serve.

This salad goes very well with all grilled meats, substantial meat dishes, and fried fish.

Preparation time: 20 minutes
Finishing time: 5 minutes

Scarole with Nut Sauce

1 head scarole

2 shallots

50 grams/2 oz salted cashew nuts or peanuts

3 tablespoons lemon juice

2 tablespoons dry sherry (fino)

3 tablespoons walnut oil

salt, 1 pinch sugar

black pepper

1 bunch flat-leaved parsley

Clean the scarole. Remove sufficient of the stalk that all the leaves fall away from each other. Wash the leaves, drain and spin dry, then cut into 2 cm/1 inch wide strips. Peel and chop the shallots. Chop

the nuts finely in a food processor, or liquidiser. Mix them with the lemon juice, sherry and walnut oil, and season with the salt, sugar and pepper.
Mix the salad with the sauce. Rinse, dry and chop the parsley. Sprinkle it, with the chopped shallots over the top of the salad, and only mix together at the table.

This salad goes well with all game dishes, roast red meats, and strongly flavoured boiled fish dishes.

Preparation time: 15 minutes
Finishing time: 5 minutes

Curly Endive with Herb-Cream

1 head curly endive

1 small garden cucumber

1 bunch mixed seasonal herbs

1 clove garlic

2 egg yolks

10 ml/⅓ fl oz sour cream

2 tablespoons mild herb vinegar

salt, white pepper from mill

1 pinch sugar

Clean the curly endive, cut out the stalk, wash the leaves and spin-dry.
Peel and halve the cucumber and remove the pips. Cut the cucumber into thin slices, laying some aside.
Rinse, dry and chop the herbs coarsely.
Peel and chop the clove of garlic, or pass through a garlic press.
Pass the egg yolks through a sieve, mix with the sour cream and vinegar to make a smooth

sauce, and season with salt, pepper and sugar.
Mix two-thirds of the herbs with the garlic.

Pull the salad into bite-sized pieces and mix together with the sauce and cucumber in a bowl. Garnish with the reserved cucumber slices and season these with a little salt and sprinkle with the remaining herbs.

This salad tastes especially good with poached fish fillets, "truite au bleu", or any fish cooked "a la meunière", meat and potato puddings, and stewed red meats.

Preparation time: 15 minutes
Finishing time: 5 minutes

15

Endive and Radicchio

Both of these are newcomers to the chicory family as their bitter flavour indicates. Nevertheless the relationship is somewhat lengthy. Endive, which appears as a white-yellow shoot grown in the dark, first made its appearance in 1845 at the Botanical Gardens in Brussels as a horti-cultural secret. It is not clear, even to this day, whether the success of this plant was arrived at by design or accident. It is possible, however, that this so-beloved salad-stuff arose in some dark cellar of a forgotten endive root which began to grow. Radicchio, on the other hand, is a leaf-salad, which originated in the northern Italian region of Veneto. It has been called by a local poet "Un fiore che si mangia" (a flower which can be eaten), in view of its colour which varies from a dark pinky-red almost to a violet, and its flower-like shape makes it very useful as a garnish to other salad-stuffs.

Endive and Pineapple salad

| 4 middle-sized belgian endives |
| 200 grams/7 oz canned pineapple |
| 3 tablespoons sherry vinegar |
| salt, cayenne pepper |
| 5 tablespoons walnut- or almond-oil |
| 2 tablespoons cream |
| 1 teaspoon chopped flat-leaved parsley |

Remove the outside leaves from the endives if necessary. Remove the bitter central core from each with a sharp, pointed knife. Wash the plants, drain carefully and cut into 2 cm/1 inch thick slices.
Cut the pineapple into fine dice.
Mix the sherry vinegar with the salt and cayenne pepper, then slowly mix in the oil and finally add the cream.
Mix the endive and pineapple dice with the sauce and sprinkle with the chopped parsley. Serve.

This salad goes very well with roast game of all sorts, fillet steaks, kebabs, and all whole fried fish.

Preparation time: 10 minutes
Finishing time: 3 minutes

Advice: There are endive varieties which do not contain a bitter core or bitter leaves originating in Holland and sold as pre-packed. One cannot always be sure if those endives sold "loose" are of the same type not containing this bitter element. In order to be sure, it is best to soak these endives in water for about 15 minutes, but some of the valuable minerals and vitamins may be lost, but the bitter elements are very valuable themselves to the metabolism!

Radicchio Salad, Piquant

| 4 medium-sized heads of radicchio, with roots |
| salt, 1 tablespoon sugar |
| 6 tablespoons red-wine vinegar |
| 1 red onion |
| 1 clove garlic |
| 8 sprigs of basil |
| $\frac{1}{2}$ bunch flat-leaved parsley |
| 4 tablespoons finest salad oil |
| 1 tablespoon nibbed almonds |

Cut the roots from the radic-chio, peel them thinly and cut into 5 mm/$\frac{1}{4}$ inch slices. Bring to the boil $\frac{1}{4}$ litre/9 fl oz water together with the salt, sugar and three tablespoons of the vinegar. Poach the root slices in this mixture for 5 minutes, then remove and allow to drain off.
Clean off the salad, wash the leaves well, allow to drain, then cut the biggest leaves lengthwise into quarters or halves.
Peel the onion and cut it into thin slices.
Peel the clove of garlic and press it into a puree with salt. Wash, spin dry and chop the basil and parsley leaves.
Mix the remaining vinegar with the oil, add the garlic, beating it into a sauce.

Mix the sauce into the radic-chio leaves, root slices and onion rings, sprinkle with the nibbed almonds and serve.

This salad goes well with wild-boar, either roast or stewed, with roast duck, well-flavoured grilled chicken and also with rolled pork roasts or suckling-pig.

Preparation time: 15 minutes
Finishing time: 5 minutes

Advice: If the root-parts are found to be very bitter, they can, of course be left out, or re-placed with thin slices of celery sticks.

Iceberg Lettuce and Cos Lettuce

Both belong to the family of garden lettuce, even though they have a completely different appearance.
Iceberg salad has crunchy, strong leaves of a white-green hue, tightly held in a cabbage-like shape.
Iceberg lettuce will keep well and the leaves keep separate, after preparation, making it very suitable for sumptuous salads.
Cos lettuce has long, dainty leaves which close together over the top, so that the heart remains white and tender, and is frequently used as a tossed green salad.

Iceberg Lettuce with Sherry Sauce

1 head iceberg lettuce
10 cl/3½ fl oz cream
80 grams/3 oz mayonnaise
1 untreated orange
3 cl/1 fl oz dry sherry (fino)
salt, 1 pinch cayenne pepper
1 tablespoon flaked almonds
1 teaspoon basil leaves

Remove the leaves from the stalk, discarding any thick, soft, outside leaves. Wash the salad briefly, although, if the head is very tight, it is often not necessary. Drain off and dry carefully in a kitchen cloth. Beat the cream, but not too stiffly. Mix with the mayonnaise.
Rinse the orange under running water, dry off and peel thinly. Cut the peel into 2 mm/$\frac{1}{10}$ inch wide strips and put to one side.
Squeeze the juice from the orange, mixing it with the sherry, then beat it into the mayonnaise/cream mixture. Season it with the salt and pepper.
Fry off the almond flakes in a non-stick pan until golden-brown.
Tear the salad-leaves into bite-sized pieces, do not cut them! Mix with the sauce, and sprinkle with the flaked almonds, strips of orange peel and the basil leaves.

This salad goes well with all sorts of short-roasted meats, such as saddle of lamb or hare, and with game dishes of all types.

Variation: If the salad is destined to go with white meats, poultry, or fish, then it can be made using a mild vinaigrette sauce. (see p. 29)

Cos Lettuce Salad with Cress

1 large cos lettuce
1 box mustard and cress
1 red onion
1 clove garlic
½ teaspoon strong mustard
4 tablespoons red wine vinegar
4 tablespoons cream
2 tablespoons soured cream (crème fraîche)
2 tablespoons thistle- or grapeseed-oil
salt, white pepper from mill
1 tablespoon chopped parsley

Clean the cos lettuce, washing the leaves carefully.
Drain them off, spreading them out onto kitchen tissue, then pat dry.
Wash the cress off under running water, leave to drain, then cut off the tiny leaves with kitchen scissors.
Peel the onion and garlic clove and chop finely.
Place the mustard, red-wine vinegar, cream, soured cream and oil into the bowl of a mixer and beat into a smooth, creamy sauce. An egg-whisk or balloon whisk may also be used.
Season the sauce with the salt and pepper.
Cut the salad into 2 cm/1 inch wide strips, and mix together with the cress, chopped onion and garlic, and the sauce.

Sprinkle with the chopped parsley and serve immediately.

The salad goes well with all turkey dishes, grilled chicken and escalopes of pork and veal.

Preparation time: 15 minutes
Finishing time: 5 minutes

Cabbages and other Leaves

White and red cabbage, and the tender Chinese leaf, are not simply salad vegetables, as many prefer them in their role as vegetables.

As salads they are eaten raw, and in view of their hard leaf structure red and white cabbages often need previous preparation in order to soften them before use. For this there are two methods. The first: Pour boiling water over the sliced cabbage in a pan, weighting it down with a plate or similar and leave it for 10 minutes. Drain into a colander and press out the water. The second method is to layer the cut cabbage with salt in a dish and leave it covered at room temperature for 4 hours. The salt causes the juices from the vegetable to be released and render it soft and tender. Drain it off well and dry with a kitchen tissue. If using this method, little or no salt should be used in the recipe for seasoning. Chinese leaves need little or no prior preparation in view of the tenderness of their leaves.

Red Cabbage Salad with Grapes

| 400 grams/14 oz red cabbage |
| 125 ml/4 fl oz meat stock |
| 4 tablespoons red-wine vinegar |
| 1 teaspoon coriander seeds |
| 5 pimento seeds |
| 2 cloves |
| 100 grams/$3\frac{1}{2}$ oz black dessert grapes |
| 1 sharp dessert apple (Jonathan, Granny Smith or Boskop) |
| 4 tablespoons wheat-germ oil |
| 2 tablespoons grated horseradish (commercial, from jar) |
| salt, if necessary |

Quarter the cabbage, remove the stalk and hard centre parts, then slice or cut finely. Leave to soak in boiling water, as described above.
After draining, mix quickly with the hot meat stock and the red-wine vinegar.
Grind the coriander and pimento seeds, together with the cloves in a mortar, and mix with the cabbage, which must be allowed to stand for at least 1 hour.
Wash and drain the grapes, remove the stalks, then halve them and remove the pips.
Quarter the apple, remove the core, peel and cut the flesh into fine dice.
Mix the oil and horse-radish into the salad and season with salt if necessary. Finally mix in the apple dice and grape halves.

This salad goes very well with pork and ham roasts as well as meat loaves and substantial grills.

Preparation time: (excluding marinating time) 25 minutes
Finishing time: 5 minutes

Note: If children are to partake of this salad omit the horse-radish and place a small bowl of it on the table for diners to add some should they wish.

White Cabbage Salad with Raisins

| 500 grams/18 oz white cabbage |
| $\frac{1}{2}$ teaspoon each of caraway and pimento seeds |
| 2 teaspoons salt |
| 2 red onions |
| 2 thin leeks |
| 2 slices of canned pineapple |
| 50 grams/2 oz seedless raisins |
| 2 beakers cream yoghurt (each 175 grams/6 oz) |
| 2 tbspns finest salad oil |
| salt, white pepper |

Quarter and slice the white cabbage, removing the stalk and any hard parts.
Grind the caraway and pimento seeds in a mortar. Leave the cabbage to soak with salt as described above, sprinkling each layer with the spices. Peel the onions and chop finely. Clean the leek, wash if necessary and cut the light-coloured parts only into 2 mm/$\frac{1}{8}$ inch rings. Drain the pineapple and cut into small dice. Soak the raisins in hot water and drain them well.

Mix the yoghurt and oil together to make a smooth sauce, and season it with a little salt and plenty of pepper. Mix all the salad ingredients together with the sauce and leave to stand for 10 minutes, adding some more salt, if necessary.

The salad goes well with all substantial roasts, goulash, roast duck and boiled beef.

Preparation time: (excluding marinading time) 20 minutes
Finishing time: 5 minutes

Chinese Leaf Salad

| 600 grams/21 oz Chinese leaf |
| 2 oranges |
| 2 mandarins |
| 4 tablespoons lemon juice |
| 1 teaspoon sugar, salt |
| 2 tablespoons thistle- or grape-seed oil |

Cut the Chinese leaf lengthwise, wash, drain well and cut across finely, like noodles. Peel the orange with a knife, like an apple, down to the flesh, in order to remove the white inner pith, then cut out the segments with a sharp knife, without removing the membrane between the segments.
Peel the mandarins, and remove the skin from the segments.
Mix the lemon juice with the sugar and salt, then mix in the oil.
Mix all the salad ingredients together in a bowl and leave to stand before serving for about 5 minutes.

Preparation time: 15 minutes
Finishing time: 5 minutes

21

Tomatoes and Cucumbers

Both the beef-steak and the round tomatoes are equally suited to be used for salads, and are obtainable throughout the year from domestic sources or imports, being grown out-doors in the summer months, and in glass-houses at other times of the year, the best-known (in Europe) coming from Holland, The Canary Islands, Italy, Spain etc.

The glass-house product is very good, but lacks the intensive flavour of the sun-ripened open-air tomato. Cucumbers also appear the whole-year round from the same sources as tomatoes, and the same comment regarding flavour holds good.

The skin should only be eaten if it can be established that cucumbers have been produced without use of harmful sprays, otherwise they should be peeled. It is true that the majority of the vitamins and mineral salts are contained in the peel, but also the residues of fertilisers and those from the atmosphere.

Simple Tomato Salad

500 grams/18 oz firm slicing tomatoes

1 onion, or 3 shallots

2 tablespoons herb vinegar

1 knife-point of strong mustard

1 large pinch of salt

1 pinch sugar

6 tablespoons cold-pressed (virgin) olive-oil

pepper from mill

1 teaspoon chopped chives

Plunge the tomatoes momentarily into boiling water, then skin and slice them across, removing the eyes with a sharp knife.
Peel and chop the onion or shallots finely.
Mix the mustard, salt and sugar together with the vinegar, then beat in the oil.
Mix the sauce with the tomatoes, and season well with the pepper. Sprinkle with the chopped chives.

This salad goes well with lamb or mutton dishes, hamburger, meat loaf, or grilled meats.

Preparation time: 10 minutes
Finishing time: 5 minutes

Variation: The salad may also be seasoned with garlic, and the following herbs all go well with tomatoes: basil, borage, flat and curly parsley, chervil, lovage and dill.

Cucumber Salad

1 large salad cucumber

1 small onion, or 2 shallots

$\frac{1}{2}$ bunch dill

1—2 sprigs tarragon

1 small carton of soured cream (crème fraîche) (100 grams/ $3\frac{1}{2}$ fl oz)

2 tablespoons herb vinegar

2 tablespoons wheat-germ oil

salt, black pepper from mill

1 pinch sugar

Peel the washed salad cucumber. Taste the ends, and if bitter, they must be removed. Cut the cucumber into 2 mm/ $\frac{1}{10}$ inch thick slices.
Peel the onion or shallots and chop finely.
Wash the dill and tarragon, spin-dry and cut the dill very finely. Pull the tarragon leaves from the stalks and chop finely.
Mix the soured cream with the vinegar and oil, and season with the salt, and sugar.
Mix the onion or shallot with half of the herbs. Mix the cucumber with the sauce and sprinkle with the remaining herbs.

This salad goes well with poached fillets of fish, fish-cakes, boiled briskets of beef, pot-roasts of all kinds, and roast mutton.

Preparation time: 10 minutes
Finishing time: 5 minutes

23

Dandelion Salad

Dandelion leaves can be picked by anyone in the Spring, though preferably not in the vicinity of a motorway, or they can be bought from a good greengrocer as cultivated salad vegetables. The cultivated varieties are popular in both France and Italy and are exported from both countries. The French are dark-green in colour, while the Italians prefer the yellow-white blanched types.
The leaves can be blanched easily by placing black polythene sheeting over the plants, or, as a tip for the home cultivator, an old roofing tile placed over the plants to keep out the light will serve just as well.
Cultivated dandelion leaves are always very long. The darker sorts contain more bitter elements than the light, and the lighter the colour, the lower the vitamin and mineral salt content of the leaves. Therefore, this must be augmented by adding herbs to the salad. In spite of that, if one finds the taste of the darker, richer leaves too strong, the bitterness (and inevitably some of the valuable food value) can be reduced by blanching the leaves momentarily in boiling water.

400 grams/14 oz cultivated dandelion leaves, or 250 grams/90 oz wild dandelion leaves
2 hard-boiled eggs
1 teaspoon herb mustard
3 tablespoons red-wine- or herb-vinegar
6 tablespoons finest salad-oil
salt
white pepper from the mill
1 pinch sugar
1 small onion, or 2 shallots
½ bunch mixed seasonal herbs

Clean the dandelion leaves, wash them and dry them, in a salad drier or spin-drier.
If cultivated, cut the stalks into 1 cm/½ inch strips and tear the leaves into bite-sized pieces. If wild, tear the whole into pieces.
Shell the eggs and chop the whites finely, putting them to one side.
Pass the yolks through a sieve and mix into a creamy sauce with the mustard, vinegar and oil. Season with the salt and pepper. Peel the onion or shallots and chop finely. Wash drain and dry the herbs, then chop finely. Mix the salad with the sauce and half the onion or shallots. Put all into a serving dish, then sprinkle with the egg white, the rest of the onion and the remaining herbs. Mix only when at the table.

Dandelion leaves go especially well with roast lamb and mutton, or strong game dishes, such as wild boar, or venison, pot-roasted beef, or solid pork roasts.

Preparation time: 20 minutes
Finishing time: 5 minutes

Variations: Dandelion salad can be prepared equally well with spinach leaves, or Lamb's lettuce (see pp. 12/13), and with fried bacon, using the hot bacon fat, with the vinegar to make a hot sauce, which must be poured over the salad immediately, after which the salad is sprinkled with chopped parsley.

Wild Herb Salad

75 grams/2½ oz sorrel
75 grams/2½ oz tender dandelion leaves
75 grams/2½ oz watercress
50 grams/2 oz stinging nettle leaves
75 grams/2½ oz nasturtium leaves
50 grams/2 oz wild garlic (can be replaced with 2 cloves garlic)
1 egg yolk
½ teaspoon mustard
3 tablespoons vinegar
salt, white pepper from mill
6 tablespoons thistle oil
1–2 tablespoons dry white wine

Check all the leaves thoroughly, then wash well and spin-dry. Cut the large leaves into bite-sized pieces. Wash the wild garlic stems, dab them dry and cut into thin rings. If using the garlic cloves, peel them and chop finely. Strain the egg yolk and mix with the mustard, vinegar, salt, pepper, followed by the oil, and the white wine if desired.

Mix the salad with the sauce
and serve at once.

This salad goes well with
game dishes, fillet of beef, and
with all game birds.

Preparation time: 25 minutes
Finishing time: 5 minutes

Basic Dressings

Redcurrant Dressing

½ quantity of mayonnaise—see recipe p. 27

2 tablespoons redcurrant jelly

1 teaspoon freshly-grated horseradish

grated rind and juice of ½ untreated orange

a little lemon juice

1 pinch salt

1 generous pinch English mustard powder

2 tablespoons cream

Mix the mayonnaise, redcurrant jelly, horse-radish, together with the peel and juice of the orange.
Season with the lemon juice, salt, and mustard powder, finally mixing in the cream.
Variation: Add a little stewed apple purée to the sauce, replacing the mustard powder with ground paprika. This sauce would go well with fish salads.

Cream Dressing

4 tablespoons freshly-squeezed lemon juice

½ teaspoonful strong mustard

salt, 1 pinch sugar

black pepper from mill

⅛ litre/5 fl oz cream

Mix the lemon juice with the mustard, and season with the salt, sugar and pepper.
Beat the cream half-stiff and beat in the lemon juice little by little. In this way the sauce will not go runny, but stay smooth and creamy.
Variation: If 3 tablespoons of mayonnaise are beaten into this cream sauce then the dressing is known as Chantilly sauce.

Roquefort Dressing

125 grams/4½ oz Roquefort cheese

6 tablespoons cold-pressed olive oil

2 tablespoons wine- or sherry-vinegar

black pepper from mill

Break up the Roquefort well with a fork.
Beat the oil and vinegar together until creamy
and add little by little to the cheese until the
whole mixture becomes smooth.
Season the sauce to taste with the pepper.
Variation: If a milder sauce is desired, use
Gorgonzola cheese instead of Roquefort. If a
creamier consistency is needed, add some
soured cream (crème fraîche). This latter makes
it ideal to go with fruit-based salads.
Note: Roquefort sauce is often falsely called
"French Dressing". In fact, in classical cuisine
this is made from oil and vinegar only seasoned
with salt and pepper together with a little
French mustard (Moutarde de Dijon).

Mayonnaise

2 egg yolks, 1 pinch of salt

1 teaspoon freshly squeezed lemon juice

1 teaspoon strong mustard

½ litre/18 fl oz olive- or wheat-germ oil

Have the egg yolks at room temperature and
remove the white strands.
Place the yolks together with some of the salt
and a few drops of lemon juice into a bowl and
beat together with a balloon whisk into a
homogeneous mass. Beat the oil in well, at first
drop by drop, then in a thin stream, preferably
with a hand whisk. Before finishing, add the
rest of the lemon juice and some more salt if
necessary.
Note: Mayonnaise always comes out better
if all ingredients are at room temperature. If a
larger quantity of mayonnaise is needed, it
should be made using a mixer or blender.
Mayonnaise can be kept in the refrigerator for
up to 14 days, if well closed.

Russian Dressing

1 recipe Thousand Island dressing	
$\frac{1}{4}$ finely chopped beetroot	
$\frac{1}{2}$ bunch chives	
1 teaspoon chopped parsley	
1 teaspoon caviar	

Mix the Thousand Island dressing with the beetroot (raw or cooked).
Rinse off the chives, dab dry and chop, adding with the parsley to the dressing.
Mix in the caviar only just before serving.
Note: German caviar is actually the cheapest, but gives the dressing a slightly les attractive appearance. If genuine caviar is too good or too dear to be used, then red or yellow salmon caviar, or dark trout caviar can be used instead.

Plaza Dressing

2 tablespoons mango chutney	
3 tablespoons tarragon vinegar	
$\frac{1}{2}$ teaspoon English mustard powder	
salt	
5 tablespoons cold-pressed olive oil (virgin olive oil) or grapeseed oil	

Chop the mango chutney finely.
Mix the vinegar together with the mustard powder and salt.
Add the oil, drop by drop adding the chutney last of all.
This dressing goes very well with meat and egg salads, as well as salads containing boiled fish.

Classical Vinaigrette

1 bunch of seasonal herbs (at least parsley, chervil, chives and tarragon)

1–2 shallots

2 hard-boiled egg yolks

2 tablespoons herb vinegar

$\frac{1}{2}$ teaspoon strong mustard, salt

black pepper from mill

5 tablespoons cold-pressed olive oil (virgin olive oil)

Wash the herbs, dry well and chop.
Chop the peeled shallots finely.
Pass the egg yolk through a sieve and mix in the vinegar and mustard, seasoning with the salt and pepper.
Mix in the oil little by little, adding the chopped herbs at the end.
Variation: The sauce can be given more flavour by adding a few chopped capers and a couple of finely-chopped anchovy fillets. Then the sauce goes extremely well with salads made from boiled fish or meat.

Thousand Island Dressing

$\frac{1}{2}$ small red capsicum

$\frac{1}{2}$ small green capsicum

1 shallot, or finely chopped onion

50 grams/2 oz mayonnaise

4 tablespoons sour cream

salt, ground sweet paprika, chili sauce

Chop the washed and cleaned capsicums very finely. Chop the peeled shallot likewise.
Mix the mayonnaise and sour cream together, flavouring with the salt, paprika and chili sauce, mixing in the chopped capsicums and shallot last of all.
This dressing may be made containing fewer calories if the mayonnaise is substituted by yoghurt, or curd cheese thinned with a little milk if necessary. If this is used, a pinch of sugar may be added.

29

Cooked Vegetables as a Gourmet's Salad

Many kinds of vegetables both raw and cooked can be used to advantage to add originality and variety.

Celeriac Salad

Celeriac is available on the home market (in Europe) from October to April, and thanks to its richness in vitamins and minerals it is a valuable winter vegetable. The strongly-flavoured oils it contains, together with its relation, celery, make it a prized soup vegetable, or flavouring for stews.

As a vegetable accompaniment to a main dish it is less prized but finds its own place as a salad vegetable, and here in its cooked state rather than raw, and if raw, only finely grated, or cut into julienne.

2 small heads of celeriac (each about 300 grams/11 oz) with a little of the leaves left on

4 tablespoons herb- or wine-vinegar

salt

1 teaspoon dill seeds

1 large pinch sugar

black pepper from the mill

1 large sharp apple (e.g. Boskop, or Granny Smith)

5 tablespoons preferred salad oil (walnut oil is very good)

Cut off the tender leaves from the celeriac and reserve. Scrub the roots well under running water, then peel them. Take ¾ litre/26 fl oz water with 2 tablespoons vinegar, 1 teaspoon salt and the dill seeds and bring to the boil in a pan.

Put in the celeriac and cook for about 20 minutes until it is just cooked, so that it is still very firm. Drain the roots and wash off under lukewarm water to ensure that there are no dill seeds still sticking to them. Halve or quarter them then cut them into thin slices with a decorating knife.

From 2 tablespoons of the strained cooking liquor, the remaining vinegar, sugar and pepper, make up a piquant sauce.

Quarter, peel and core the apple and grate it coarsely. Mix it quickly with the celeriac and the sauce, and let it stand together for 20 minutes.

Wash the leaves from the celeriac, dry well and chop finely. Mix into the salad together with the oil. Season with salt, if necessary, and serve.

This salad goes very well with grilled or fried pork, roast game of all kinds and with roast goose or roast duck. In North Germany it is usually served with the minced meat dish known as "Falscher Hase" (Mock Hare), and with pot-roasted beef.

Preparation time: (without cooking and cooling time) 15 minutes
Finishing time: 10 minutes

Beetroot Salad

Beetroot from the kitchen garden are at their most plentiful in September and October, but are obtainable the whole year round from one source or another, although sometimes scarce and expensive. They can be purchased either raw or cooked, or peeled, vacuum-packed ready-to-eat.

They fall nicely into the group of root vegetables which are seldom eaten raw, but mostly as salads, and especially as a pickle or conserve, in vinegar, but if bought raw and cooked before peeling there will be minimal vitamin and mineral-salt losses. The soft inner leaves may be blanched and used in salads, as they contain much iron.

600 grams/1¼ lbs raw beet-roots (small roots) with leaves on
1 teaspoon caraway seeds
1 teaspoon dill or fennel seeds
8 tablespoons herb- or red-wine-vinegar
1 small onion
1 small clove garlic
½ bunch mixed seasonal herbs
½ teaspoon strong mustard
1 pinch sugar
white pepper from mill
8 tablespoons finest salad oil

Remove the leaves from the roots without cutting into the flesh of the roots in order to prevent the beets from "bleeding".

Bring 1 litre/35 fl oz water to the boil with the caraway seeds, dill or fennel seeds, 1 tablespoon salt and 4 tablespoons vinegar. Put in the beetroots and let them simmer, covered with a lid, for 25 minutes.
Drain them off, refresh under cold running water, and peel immediately.
Slice with a decorating knife into 1 mm/1/16 inch thick slices and allow to cool.
Peel the onion and clove of garlic and chop them finely, together with the previously washed and dried herbs.
From the remaining vinegar, mustard, sugar, salt and pepper, make up a piquant sauce, beating in the oil with a balloon whisk, and adding a little of the cooking liquor, if desired.
Mix the beetroot with the sauce; wash and dry the most tender beetroot leaves and chop them. Put the salad into a serving dish and sprinkle the top with the leaves.

This salad goes well with game dishes of all types, boiled beef and grilled pig's feet (Schweinshaxe).

Preparation time: (without time for cooking and cooling)
25 minutes
Finishing time: 5 minutes

33

Fennel Salad

Fennel has its origins in Persia and the Mediterranean area. Formerly an important flavouring plant, it is now treasured more as a vegetable. It has taken much effort in the past to turn the long-stemmed umbelliferous herb plant, rich with leaves, into the turnip-rooted vegetable fennel which bears no fruits. Although the herb fennel is grown in England, most of the vegetable fennel is imported from either France or Italy. The high season for the fine, tender vegetable is from October to April, but a restricted amount is available throughout the Summer.

750 grams/1 lb 10 oz small fennel roots
$\frac{1}{10}$ litre/5 fl oz dry white wine
salt
1 teaspoon sugar
$\frac{1}{2}$ bunch flat-leaved parsley
3 tablespoons wine vinegar
4 tablespoons cold-pressed olive oil (virgin olive oil)
black pepper from mill

Cut off the hard stalk and the leaves from the fennel. Put the leaves to one side.
Clean the fennel, cut into halves and remove the hard centre core.
Put $\frac{1}{2}$ litre/18 fl oz water into a pan, with plenty of salt and the sugar, bring to the boil and add the fennel. Cover and cook on a medium heat for 15 minutes until it is half-cooked. Drain into a colander and allow to cool.
Wash the parsley and the fennel leaves, spin-dry and chop them finely.

Cut the fennel halves lengthwise into 4 strips and arrange on a deep dish.
Pour over the vinegar and oil, sprinkle with the herbs and season well with the pepper. The salad goes best with poached or fried fish, light roast, veal or pork escalopes, fried sweetbreads or grilled scampi.

Preparation time: 10 minutes
Finishing time: (without time for cooking or cooling) 5 minutes

Variation: Fennel can also be used raw. It is then cleaned, washed and halved after which the roots are cut across in thin slices and dressed with just a simple Vinaigrette Dressing (see p. 29) or a Cream Dressing (see p. 26). Sprinkle with the chopped green fennel leaves. This salad goes well with all fish dishes.

Note: Do not throw fennel trimmings away, but clean them, wash and dry them, chop them finely and freeze them, or allow to dry. Add a little to soups and stews when needed.

Kohlrabi Salad

Kohlrabi only appears as a root, although it belongs to the stalk vegetables, between roots and leaves. It develops an apple-sized root which, according to type is either light green or mauve, the lighter coloured being usually glasshouse grown, while the darker are grown in the open. The tender centre leaves of the kohlrabi contain more mineral salts and vitamins than the kohlrabi itself and also give a discreet flavour.

3 kohlrabi (each about 200 grams/7 oz)
$\frac{1}{2}$ litre/18 fl oz strongly-flavoured meat stock
8 sprigs basil, or 8 large leaves
$\frac{1}{2}$ bunch chervil
1 sprig lemon balm
1 young carrot
10 cl/$3\frac{1}{2}$ fl oz cream
2 tablespoons lemon juice
1 tablespoon walnut oil
salt, if necessary

Remove the tender centre leaves from the kohlrabi and reserve.
Peel the kohlrabi cutting it first into slices, then into strips. Bring the stock to the boil, add the kohlrabi and blanch it for 5 minutes. Remove from the pan with a perforated spoon and allow to cool. Do not throw away the liquor (see Note below).
Wash the kohlrabi leaves, basil, chervil and lemon balm, dry well. Remove the stalks and chop the leaves finely.
Peel the carrot and grate finely or chop.
Mix the cream with the lemon juice, beat in the walnut oil and season with the salt if desired.
Mix the kohlrabi, carrot and herbs into the sauce and dress into a serving dish.

This salad goes well with all types of lightly roasted meats, breast of veal, roast pork, all lamb and mutton dishes, as well as poached fish.

Preparation time: 5 minutes
Finishing time: (without cooking and cooling time) 20 minutes

Variation: For using raw kohlrabi roots, prepare as above, but grate coarsely and mix with a Roquefort Dressing (see p. 27). Sprinkle with the chopped kohlrabi leaves and chopped parsley. Goes well with poached or fried fish, as well as roast loin of veal or pork.

Note: Do not throw away the cooking liquor from the kohlrabi, but use it the following day as a basis for a cream of kohlrabi soup. Add a peeled chopped kohlrabi root with 1 or 2 leeks cut into rings. Cook off the vegetables in the stock, purée the whole with a blender and add cream and/or milk to the required quantity. Heat again and add nutmeg to taste.

Cauliflower Salad with Curry Sauce

Cauliflower is one of the most popular vegetables and is normally prepared in the simplest ways.

1 cauliflower (about 750 grams/26 oz)

salt

1 teaspoon sugar

5 peppercorns

1 small red capsicum

2 spring onions (scallions)

100 grams/3½ oz mayonnaise

2 tablespoons cream

1 tablespoon lemon juice

1 tablespoon curry powder

1 pinch ground coriander seeds

25 grams/¾ oz coarsely chopped hazelnuts

a few coriander or chervil leaves

Clean the cauliflower and split up into florets. Wash well and allow to drain.
Bring 1 litre/35 fl oz water to the boil with the peppercorns. Lay in the cauliflower florets and cook for 10 minutes until just cooked (al dente).
Clean and wash the capsicum, then cut into halves across, then cut into very thin strips lengthways.
Clean the spring onions. Chop the white finely and cut the green into thin rings.
Take the cauliflower florets out of the water with a skimmer and place in a colander, or allow to dry on a thick layer of kitchen tissue. Allow to cool.
Mix the mayonnaise together with the cream, lemon juice, curry powder and season with the coriander and salt if necessary.
Mix the cauliflower florets carefully with the spring onion and the capsicum strips and fold the sauce in gently. Sprinkle with the hazelnuts and either coriander or chervil leaves.

This salad will go well with all types of roasted meats, red or white, turkey joints, or poached fish.

Preparation time: (without time for cooling) 25 minutes
Finishing time: 5 minutes

Note: Do not discard the stalks from cauliflower or broccoli, as they can be made into the basis for a cream soup if peeled, cooked and puréed.

Broccoli Salad

Broccoli is not, as many suppose, a more refined form of the white cauliflower, more its precursor. It developed centuries ago in Asia Minor early in the process of cultivating the wild cauliflower into the white variety that we know today.

750 grams/26½ oz broccoli

salt

4 tablespoons wine vinegar

1 teaspoon strong mustard

1 large pinch of sugar

black pepper from the mill

2 hard-boiled eggs

6 tablespoons oil

1 bunch mixed seasonal herbs (or 1 packet of deep-frozen mixed herbs)

4 tomatoes

½ bunch radishes

2 slices toasting bread

10 grams/⅓ oz butter

1 clove garlic

Clean the broccoli, cutting off the hardest parts of the stalks. Peel the stalks and cut a cross into the stalks so that the stalks and the flower heads will cook at the same time.
Boil plenty of salted water in a pan and lay in the broccoli, cooking it for 10–12 minutes until it is still very firm (al dente). Take it out with a skimmer and refresh quickly in cold water. Allow to drain and lay it on a thick layer of kitchen tissue to cool completely.

In the meantime, prepare the sauce. Mix together the vinegar, mustard, sugar, salt and pepper. Shell the eggs, passing the yolks through a sieve and chopping the whites finely. Put to one side.

Mix the egg yolks and the oil into the vinegar. Wash the herbs, spin-dry and chop finely. If using deep-frozen herbs, allow to defrost first. Mix into the sauce.

Blanch the tomatoes, skin them, removing the pips and the core. Cut the flesh into thin strips. Top and tail the radishes, then wash and quarter them.

Cut the broccoli into florets, cutting the stalk ends into 1 cm/½ inch thick slices. Mix the broccoli, radishes and tomato strips into the sauce and place the whole into a bowl.

Cut off the crusts from the bread. Place the butter in a pan and fry off the bread slices until they are golden-brown on each side. Peel and half the garlic clove and rub the cut faces well into the fried bread, before cutting it into tiny cubes.

Place the salad into a serving dish, sprinkling it with the egg white and croutons.

This salad goes well with grilled meats, such as rump or fillet steaks, roast chicken, roast minced veal loaf, game stews, and lamb cutlets.

Preparation time: (without cooking time) 15 minutes
Finishing time: 15 minutes

Variation: Instead of garlic croutons, diced crisply-fried streaky (belly) smoked bacon can be used, or roasted, flaked almonds, or salted peanuts.

Brussels Sprout Salad

Brussels sprouts are the most tasty winter vegetables of our latitude, and like green cabbage are improved in flavour by a light frost. Traditionally, outdoor Brussels sprouts were never harvested before the first frosts of winter. Many stories are told about Brussels sprouts, but the most probable is that the Brussels sprout, like the Belgian endive (chicory) was a result of intensive cultivation by a clever gardener in Brussels. More than 120 years have passed since their introduction and they are known in French as "Choux de Bruxelles", as in English, but in German as "Rosenkohl" (rose cabbage).

500 grams/18 oz tightly closed Brussels sprouts
$\frac{1}{2}$ litre/18 fl oz strongly flavoured meat stock
1 beetroot
2 carrots
100 grams/$3\frac{1}{2}$ oz celeriac
2 spring onions
1 bunch flat-leaved parsley
1 carton soured cream (crème fraîche) 200 grams/7 oz
salt, black pepper from mill
grated nutmeg

Clean the Brussels sprouts by taking off any wilting or yellowed leaves, then cutting off the stalk level at the base. Wash them well and allow to drain. Cut a cross into the base of the stalk.

Bring the meat stock to the boil in a pan and put in the Brussels sprouts, bringing the pan back to the boil, covering with a lid, and cooking the sprouts for 8–10 minutes on a medium heat, until cooked, but very firm (al dente). Take out of the pan with a skimmer and place in a bowl.
Scrub off the beetroot well with a brush, place it into a pan with cold water and cook for 15–20 minutes. Peel the carrot and the celeriac and cut them into fine strips. They can be cooked in the meat stock after the removal of the sprouts for 5 minutes until they are just cooked also, then drain them off. Clean off the spring onions, then chop the white parts and cut the green into fine circles. Peel the beetroot and cut it into thin strips

also. Wash and dry the parsley then chop finely. Mix all the salad ingredients together with the soured cream, seasoning them with the salt, pepper, and nutmeg.
The salad can be served warm, if desired.

This salad goes very well with game dishes of all kinds, roast pheasant, as well as roast goose and duck.

Preparation time: 20 minutes
Finishing time: (without cooking time) 10 minutes

Brussels Sprout Salad with Walnuts

Cook the cleaned Brussels sprouts in plenty of salted water for 8–10 minutes, drain them and allow to cool.

From 4 tablespoons sherry vinegar, $\frac{1}{2}$ teaspoon strong mustard, salt, white pepper from the mill, some ground coriander and 6 tablespoons walnut oil prepare a sauce. Mix the salad into it and allow to stand for 20 minutes. Sprinkle the top with 50 grams/2 oz of chopped walnuts, and the sieved yolk of 1 hard-boiled egg.

This salad goes well with game and also with suckling pig.

Preparation time: 15 minutes
Finishing time: (without cooking and cooling time) 10 minutes

Brussels Sprouts in Chestnut Sauce

Cook the smallest possible Brussels sprouts until just done in plenty of boiling water, seasoned with salt, pepper and nutmeg for 6–8 minutes, then drain and allow to cool.

Mix together 100 grams/$3\frac{1}{2}$ oz canned chestnut purée with 4 tablespoons of soured cream (crème fraîche). Add 2 finely chopped shallots and 2 tablespoons dry sherry (fino) and mix well together.

If desired, the salad may be finished off with ground coloured peppers and chopped chervil leaves.

This salad will enrich fillet of pork, roast game birds, haunch of venison, or roast beef.

Preparation time: 15 minutes
Finishing time: (without cooking and cooling time) 10 minutes

43

Asparagus

To connoisseurs, asparagus is the king of vegetables.
The thick, white-fleshed asparagus comes from a strain having its origins in the East, and found great favour in ancient Egypt, Greece and Rome. The green asparagus by contrast is a refined form of a North African wild plant. From it one can eat only the longish head and a little of the stem, as the lower parts are hard and bitter.

Asparagus and Mushroom Salad

500 grams/18 oz white asparagus

½ teaspoonful sugar

salt

5 grams/⅕ oz butter

200 grams/7 oz small boletus mushrooms

juice of 1 lemon

½ teaspoon coriander seeds

3 tablespoons raspberry vinegar

6 tablespoons walnut or grapeseed oil

½ box mustard and cress

Wash and peel the asparagus then trim the bottom ends of the stems.
Put the peelings into a long pan fitted with a strainer insert together with ⅛ litre/4 fl oz water. Place in the strainer and lay the asparagus on to it. Sprinkle it with the sugar, salt and pieces of the butter. Close the pan well and steam the asparagus for 20–25 minutes. They should, in any case be still very firm (al dente). Drain the asparagus and allow to cool.
In the meantime, clean the

44

mushrooms. In the process, using a sharp knife, get rid of any roots, rubbing them off with a kitchen cloth. Slice them using an egg slicer, putting the slices immediately into a bowl containing the lemon juice, mixing them round in the juice, so that the slices do not discolour. Grind the coriander seeds in a mortar. Cut the asparagus into lengths each about 4 cm/1½ inches long. Mix the vinegar, oil, coriander seeds and salt together. Drain the mushroom slices in a colander, then lay them on a thick layer of kitchen tissue, and pat them dry.

Mix the mushrooms, asparagus and sauce together in a serving dish. Wash off the cress, allow to drain and cut off the leaves. Sprinkle the leaves over the top of the salad and serve quickly.

This salad goes well with poached prime fish fillets, stewed veal, seafood ragouts, or fried pork fillet.

Preparation time: (without cooking time for the asparagus) 25 minutes
Finishing time: 10 minutes

Variation: Instead of mushrooms, florets of cooked, cooled broccoli can be mixed with the asparagus, in which case, substitute the coriander for a touch of black pepper from the mill, and the raspberry vinegar for sherry- or a good wine-vinegar.

Green Asparagus Salad

600 grams/21 oz green asparagus
salt
1 pinch white pepper
1 hard-boiled egg yolk
½ bunch chervil
6 stalks or 6 large leaves basil
4 tablespoons sherry- or wine-vinegar
½ teaspoon strong mustard
6–7 tablespoons cold-pressed olive oil (virgin olive oil)

Carefully wash the asparagus in cold water. Cut off the woody ends of the stalks with a sharp knife. Peel the asparagus carefully from tip to bottom. Put plenty of water into a pan, salt well and season with pepper. Bring to the boil, putting in the asparagus and cooking it for a bare 10 minutes. Pour off the water, drain and allow to cool somewhat.

In the meantime, chop the hard-boiled egg yolk coarsely, wash the chervil and basil, dry them and chop them finely. Mix the vinegar and mustard together, then beat in the oil drop by drop.
Season with a little salt.
Put the asparagus into an oval dish pouring over the sauce. Sprinkle with the chopped herbs and hard-boiled egg yolk.
This salad tastes good with red meats of any sort, grilled scampi, fried breast of chicken, and also roast beef.

Preparation time: (without cooking or cooling time) 25 minutes
Finishing time: 10 minutes

45

Italian-Style Bean Salad

For this fine salad a fine type of bean should be chosen. Especially good are the tender princess beans, a special kind of bush or runner bean. A slightly larger top-quality bean, or the tender Kenya bean may also be used.

500 grams/18 oz green beans

salt

2 stalks fresh or dried savory

4 stalks fresh or dried thyme

1 clove garlic

1 shallot

4 tablespoons finest wine vinegar

1 pinch sugar

white pepper from the mill

6–7 tablespoons cold-pressed olive oil (virgin olive oil)

75 grams/3 oz Mozzarella cheese

6 stalks or 6 large leaves basil

1 tablespoon each of pine kernels and chopped pistachio nuts

Clean, wash and drain the beans. Bring plenty of well-salted water to the boil in a pan, together with the savory and thyme. Put in the beans and cook for 6–8 minutes, until just cooked. Put the beans into a colander, refresh with cold water and allow to drain, naturally removing the savory and thyme.
Peel and chop finely the shallot and garlic clove.
Mix the wine vinegar together with some salt, sugar and a little pepper. Beat in the oil drop by drop. Mix the beans with the sauce, garlic and shallots and leave to stand for 10 minutes.
In the meantime, dice the Mozzarella finely. Rinse off the basil, dab it dry, then cut into thin strips, or chop, then sprinkle it, with the chopped herbs over the top of the salad.

This salad goes well with roast chicken or turkey, pot-roasted beef, roast beef, or grilled or fried whole fish.

Preparation time: 20 minutes
Finishing time: (without cooling or standing time) 15 minutes

Broad Bean Salad

Here and there one can find ready-shelled broad beans in delicatessen stores, but it is better to indulge in the time-consuming task to obtain the tender end product, which is well worth while!

1 kilo/$2\frac{1}{4}$ lbs broad beans

salt

4 stalks savory

4 shallots or 2 small onions

1 small carrot

5 grams/$\frac{1}{6}$ oz butter

4 tablespoons dry white wine

4 tablespoons cream

2 tablespoons soured cream (crème fraîche)

2 tablespoons lemon juice

1 small pinch ground coriander seed

1 small head oak-leaf lettuce

$\frac{1}{2}$ box mustard and cress

Top and tail the beans. Bring to the boil a pan with plenty of salted water and the savory. Put in the beans and cook for about 6 minutes until they are firm to the touch.

Drain them into a colander and refresh under cold water, then strip off the hard outer skin. Allow the shelled beans to cool.

Peel the shallots or onions, chop finely and fry off in the butter. Moisten with the wine, and cook off briefly, then allow to cool.

Peel the carrot and cut it into julienne (fine strips). Mix the cream, soured cream, lemon juice and the shallot mixture together. Season with salt and the coriander. Clean the lettuce, pull to pieces, wash thoroughly, spin-dry, then halve it lengthwise. Arrange it in a star shape on a serving dish. Wash the cress and drain it well. Cut off the leaves, mixing them with the carrot strips and the beans. Heap this mixture on the lettuce and pour over the sauce.

This salad goes well with all tender white roast meats, lamb cutlets, saddle of lamb, fried or poached fillets of fish, or any seafood.

Preparation time: 25 minutes
Finishing time: 15 minutes

Pepper Salad or Capsicum Salad

Peppers or capsicums have conquered Europe from two sides. At the beginning of the 16th century, the Spaniards brought the so-called Ecuadorian form from Central and South America to Spain, while at about the same time, the Oriental form found its way via Turkey to Hungary. Like the tomato, the pepper or capsicum plant was first brought over to interest the rich as an ornamental shrub. The Hungarians soon noticed what a culinary delicacy they had collected in their simple flowerpots and cultivated the capsicum both as a spice and a vegetable.

The vegetable capsicum, according to ripeness comes in different colours, through light green, green, through yellow to red. These colours can also be determined by the type. In between, in Holland, other types have been developed which appear from light-yellow to dark-violet.

The degree of strength of the pods also depends on the sort. There are very small very strong green and light-yellow pods as well as very mild in similar colours. Nearly always, the most mild are the large fleshy green and red pods. The skins of most types of capsicums are very hard and not easily digested by some, so in making salads, they should always be previously skinned.

The best method of doing this is as follows:
Place the unwashed pods in a previously heated oven at 250°C (500°F) or gas mark 9, or under a very hot grill, and roast them until the skin appears wrinkled and possibly with little brown blisters. The pods should then be covered with a damp cloth and left to cool for about 5 minutes, when the skin can be removed easily.
The pods can then be cut or broken open. The stalk and the seedhead may then be taken out and any loose seeds removed with a spoon. It is always best to work over a plate so that any juice which may run out can be saved for use later in the sauce.

2 each of equal-sized red and yellow capsicums

2 large cloves of garlic

½ teaspoon salt

4 pimientos

6 black peppercorns

3 spring onions

½ bunch flat-leaved parsley

6 stalks fresh thyme

3 tablespoons herb vinegar

5 tablespoons cold-pressed olive oil (virgin olive oil)

50 grams/2 oz white sheep's milk cheese

Prepare the capsicum pods as described above, then cut into 2 cm/1 inch strips and cut them across, placing them in colours alternately on a plate. Peel the garlic cloves and chop them coarsely. Put them together with the salt, peppercorns and pimientoes into a mortar and pound them into a fine paste.

Peel the spring onions, cutting the white parts in rings and the green tops into strips. Place both on top of the capsicum pieces.
Rinse both the thyme and the parsley, and dab them dry. Chop the parsley and pull off the leaves from the thyme. Mix the vinegar and oil together with the garlic-spice paste and the juice from the capsicums into a sauce and spread it over the capsicum pieces. Sprinkle the top with the chopped parsley. Cut the cheese into the thinnest possible strips and rub them over the top of the salad.

This salad enhances all barbecued meat and fish dishes, and all Mediterranean cuisine.

Preparation time: 30 minutes
Finishing time: 10 minutes

Zucchini Salad or Courgette Salad

These tender baby vegetable marrows have not been known long on the domestic scene but their use has grown since the advent of popular travel. The wish for low-calorie diets has also played a part in ensuring their popularity as they are full of vitamins and mineral salts, but in their raw state have almost no flavour. Even when cooked they develop little flavour so that they may be added to other items without dominating them.

600 grams/21 oz courgettes/ zucchini

juice of 1 lemon

8 tablespoons cold-pressed olive oil (virgin olive oil)

1 bayleaf

1 teaspoon coriander seeds

1 teaspoon black peppercorns

salt

2 spring onions

2 cloves garlic

10 sprigs or 10 large leaves basil

2 sprigs tarragon

2 tablespoons wine vinegar

1 pinch sugar

Scrub the courgettes under running water, then cut them into slices about 1 cm/½ inch thick, cutting off both the stalk and flower end.
Put in a pan ¼ litre/9 fl oz water together with the lemon juice, 4 tablespoons oil, bayleaf, coriander seeds, peppercorns and plenty of salt and bring it to the boil.
Place in the slices of courgettes and cook for about 3 minutes. Drain into a colander, retaining the cooking liquor. Allow the courgettes to cool. In the meantime, prepare the spring onions and cut them into thin rings. Peel the cloves of garlic and chop finely.

Rinse off the basil and tarragon and dab dry. Chop them coarsely. Mix the rest of the oil with the vinegar, season with salt and sugar to taste and add some of the cooking liquor if desired. Mix the courgette rings, together with the spring onions and garlic into the sauce, place into a serving dish and sprinkle with the chopped herbs.

This salad goes well with roast chicken and all grilled meats.

Preparation time: 15 minutes
Finishing time: (without time for cooling) 15 minutes

Variations: The courgette slices can be cooked in oil instead of the stated liquor. Heat plenty of olive oil in a pan placing in the slices so that they do not overlap. Cook each side until glazed but not brown, then remove them and drain off excess fat, leaving them to cool on a layer of kitchen tissue. In this way the courgettes become very tasty, but due to the oil, very high in calories. For low calorie meals grate the washed courgettes very coarsely then prepare as described. A few black olives may be added to the salad, if desired.

Zucchini Salad with Cream Sauce

The pre-cooked or pre-fried courgettes may be mixed with a sauce made from 4 table-spoons each of soured cream (crème fraîche) and cream, to-gether with 2 tablespoons of herb vinegar. Season well with plenty of pepper and sprinkle with chopped dill weed. If desired, diced red capsicum may be mixed in.

If this salad is required to go with roast fillet of pork or saddle of veal it may be en-riched by mixing with 50 grams/2 oz of flaked tuna fish and 1 tablespoon small capers.

51

Herbs and Their Culinary Uses

Lemon Balm and Mint: Cucumber, tomatoes, fine types of fish, asparagus, white meats, sweet and savoury fruit salads.

Chervil: Same usage as mustard and cress, except for eggs, white meats, and delicate types of fish, rice and especially potatoes.

Hyssop: Tender green salads, bean and cucumber salads.

Celeriac Leaves: Potato and substantial vegetable salads.

Thyme: With green beans, tomatoes, aubergines, courgettes, rice, pasta, red meats, substantial fish dishes, Mediterranean seafood dishes,

Sorrel: With white and red meats of all sorts, all types of fish, seafood, tomatoes and cucumber.

Anise: All tender green salads, tomatoes, cucumbers.

Chives: Used in all fresh salads (except radicchio), fish and seafood, substantial meats, and potatoes.

Rosemary: Used only with strong types of meat.

Tarragon: In small quantities for use in potato and substantial vegetable salads.

Sage: Used in tiny quantities only in meat salads of Mediterranean origin.

Lovage: Used in very small amounts in tender vegetable salads.

Dill: Same usage as fennel, except for eggs.

Parsley: For all types of salads— flat-leaved parsley is finer in flavour, curly- is used mostly for decorative purposes.

Marjoram: For substantial fish and meat salads.

Mint: see Lemon Balm.

Borage: (flowers and leaves) with cucumbers, courgettes, white marrow, cos lettuce, Chinese leaves, white cabbage, strong types of fish and meat.

Mustard and Cress, or Cultivated Cress: With fine fish dishes, and all green salads. Especially good in combination with soured cream dressing, yoghurt, sour cream, and curd cheeses.

Savory: Leaves and flowers used on beans and potato salad.

Basil: tomatoes, eggs, cheese, pasta, rice, white meats, strong types of fish.

Vinegar and Oil for

A good salad is based on the following three essentials:
1. Imagination
2. First-class ingredients
3. The correct seasonings.
Points 1 and 2 are obviously stated as facts, but as regards point 3, with the exception of salt, the acid is the most important. A salad without acid is like an orchestra without a conductor – a harmonious performance cannot take place. Fortunately, the days of the pathetic vinegar or lemon juice mixtures are past. There has been a virtual revolution of connoisseurs in the realm of salad preparation. This started

some time ago in France and Italy, and has spread through Europe, and a choice of ingredients, which once were only found in the most expensive food shops is now found overall. A choice of different vinegars and oils is now on sale even in supermarkets, such as sherry or raspberry vinegar, cold-pressed olive oil, grapeseed and thistle oil.
Sherry vinegar stands at No. 1 in the scale of popularity, and the price will depend on the quality of the base wine used. For the finest salads, **raspberry vinegar** is chosen, or another fruit vinegar, **blackcurrant vinegar**, or the even finer **strawberry vinegar**. But even the

"simplest" of the sophisticated vinegars will bring honour to any salad, such as **lemon vinegar**, **herb vinegar**, **tarragon**, **shallot** or **garlic vinegar**. It is also truly important to use a good vinegar, even if one of the "first-class vinegars" is not called for, and it must be a wine vinegar. The same holds good for **red wine vinegar**. If one wishes to use the "king of vinegars", then the Italian **balsam vinegar** or "Aceto Balsamico" should be used. Aged in oak casks for years, it has a dark brown colour and a thick fluid consistency with an unparallelled flavour, and must only be used in the smallest quantities, as it is unfortunately relatively expensive. If one has to dig

he Gourmet's Kitchen

deep in one's pocket for vinegar, this is not the case in respect of oil. Although prices depend on quality, there is a great choice. In the first place we must stand by **olive oil** which has been with us for many years, and has earned a bad name due to being used widely in Mediterranean cooking, and was often of poor quality.

There are many differences in quality in olive oil, depending on the area of growth and also how the olives were pressed. Olives can be pressed several times and will yield oil at each pressing, but each will produce a poorer quality. The first cold pressing produces the so-called virgin olive oil, a product of absolute purity.

This oil is known respectively in France as "huile vierge", in Spain as "aceite virgen" and to the Italians as "olio vergine", and contains the most valuable fats that we have at our disposal. Apart from this, this virgin oil has a delicate, nutty aroma.

Nuances of flavour will depend on the area in which the olives were grown. Thus connoisseurs must find out for themselves which oil they prefer, whether it is the delicate oil from Tuscany, or the deep, green oil from the area around Rome, the strong oil from Andalucia, or from the south of France.

Whichever olive oil has the most support, there are very many who like an oil neutral in flavour, such as **soya oil**, **wheat** or **maizegerm oil**. Connoisseurs, however like to try other oils which have their own distinctive flavours and aromas, such as **sesame**, **almond**, **walnut** or **hazelnut oil**, which give properties to salad sauces which cannot be denied. **Thistle oil** can be found especially in health food shops and is considered to be extremely healthy. As it is almost tasteless, it can be used widely, as can grapeseed oil, long-used by the French in their daily cooking. Here again there are many quality differences. The best is cold-pressed with a deep green colour, which is often used in sophisticated restaurants for herb dressings.

55

A Feast to the Eye and a Pleasure to the Palate

Festive menus are unthinkable without starters to stimulate the appetite.

Gourmet's Salad

(for 6 persons)

---

150 grams/5 oz peeled fresh or deep-frozen scampi

1 boiled or grilled chicken breast (about 150 grams/5 oz)

3 kiwi fruit

1 sharon fruit (kaki or persimmon)

1 small batavia lettuce, or oak-leaf lettuce

$\frac{1}{2}$ curly endive

$\frac{1}{2}$ lettuce

2 small heads radicchio

2 shallots

100 grams/3$\frac{1}{2}$ oz fresh button mushrooms

1 avocado pear

2 tablespoons lemon juice

4 tablespoons sherry or raspberry vinegar

1 carton soured cream (crème fraîche) (without emulsifier) 200 grams/7 oz

3 tablespoons finest salad oil (cold-pressed olive oil, walnut or grapeseed oil)

2 cl/7 fl oz brandy or cognac

salt

white pepper from the mill

1 pinch sugar

6 bottled quail's eggs

Rinse off the scampi in cold water (if frozen, allow to thaw first), then drain off and dry until ready for use spread out on kitchen tissue.

Remove the skin from the chicken breast, halve lengthwise, then cut across the grain into slices 5 mm/$\frac{1}{4}$ inch thick. Peel the kiwi fruit, wash and dry the kaki, then cut it in half. Cut the kiwis into slices 5 mm/$\frac{1}{4}$ inch thick, and the kaki into 2 mm/$\frac{1}{8}$ inch thick slices.

Clean, pull to pieces and wash the four types of lettuce, then spin-dry thoroughly. Cut the long leaves only, lengthwise or across.

Peel and chop the shallots very finely.

Clean the button mushrooms and dry them in a kitchen cloth.

Peel the avocado, cut into half, remove the stone, and together with the mushrooms, cut it into thin slices.

Mix both quickly into the lemon juice so that they do not discolour.

Mix all the salad leaf pieces, half of each of the scampi and chicken breast slices, the kiwi, kaki, mushroom and avocado slices together. Sprinkle with the chopped shallots and sprinkle the mixture with 2 tablespoons of the lemon juice. Mix the soured cream with the remaining lemon juice, the oil and brandy or cognac and beat until frothy. Season with salt, pepper and sugar. Garnish the salad with the rest of the scampi and the chicken breast and the drained quails' eggs.

Place the sauce in the middle, but do not mix together until ready to eat.

This salad can be eaten as a starter with French bread or walnut bread. It is best accompanied by Muller-Thurgau or Riesling wine.

Preparation time: about 20 minutes
Finishing time: about 10 minutes

Note: Mushrooms can be cut evenly using an egg slicer, but they should not be too small. The unused halves of the chicories and the lettuce may be kept fresh if placed with a moist kitchen tissue into a polythene bag, tightly closed, and placed in a refrigerator. They can be taken out and prepared on the following day as a side salad. (see page 10).

Danicheff Salad

200 grams/7 oz celeriac

½ litre/18 fl oz meat stock

1 tablespoon vinegar

1 teaspoon sugar

250 grams/9 oz smallest possible long potatoes

salt

125 grams/4½ oz white mushrooms

1 tablespoon lemon juice

8 bottled artichoke bottoms

125 grams/4½ oz canned white asparagus tips

16 fresh or deep-frozen scampi (about 200 grams/7 oz)

150 grams/5¼ oz top-quality mayonnaise (or homemade)

3 tablespoons cream

white pepper from mill

2 hard-boiled eggs

¼ box mustard and cress

Scrub the celeriac under running water, peel and cut it into thin slices.
Heat the stock with the vinegar and sugar and cook the celeriac in it for about 10 minutes until it is cooked but still firm.
Meanwhile, peel the potatoes and cut them into 5 mm/¼ inch slices.
Put a pan to boil with plenty of salted water, then place in the potato slices and blanch them for about 5 minutes, then tip them out into a colander to drain. Allow the celeriac slices to drain in the same way, then cut them into quarters.
Clean off the mushrooms and dry them with a kitchen cloth, then remove the stalks. Cut both the heads and stalks into very thin slices and mix quickly with the lemon juice. Allow the artichoke bottoms and the asparagus tips to drain off well, then cut the artichoke bottoms into thin strips.

Put the scampi into a sieve and rinse off with cold water. (If deep-frozen, allow to thaw first.) Leave to drain, then lay them onto a thick layer of kitchen tissue to dry off, dabbing the top surface dry. Mix the mayonnaise with the cream and season with the pepper.
Mix all the prepared salad ingredients together except the scampi with the mayonnaise, and heap into a bowl. Shell the eggs and cut each into 8 segments. Garnish the salad with the scampi and the egg segments. Wash off the cress, dab dry and cut off the leaves, placing a bunch of cress in the middle of the salad. Serve the salad with thin toasted slices of French bread and a dry white wine, such as a white Burgundy.

Preparation time: (without cooling time) 35 minutes
Finishing time: 10 minutes

Danicheff salad stems from the classical cuisine, and was originally garnished with crayfish tails and truffle slices. The cress can be substituted by slices of canned truffle (about 25 grams/1 oz). If you want to use the correct crayfish for this dish instead of scampi, they should be freshwater crayfish. These taste best when there is no "r" in the month, also between May and August, but can often be obtained until February. They should be well scrubbed under running water, then placed headfirst in fast-boiling salted water, covered and cooked for 8—10 minutes. After cooling, the tail flesh should be freed from the shell. The remaining parts are not usable. Shrimps, prawns or crawfish also taste good in this salad.

Waldorf Salad

100 grams/3½ oz walnut kernels

2 sharp eating apples

juice of 1 lemon

250 grams/9 oz celeriac

10 cl/3½ fl oz cream

80 grams/3 oz finest quality mayonnaise

salt, white pepper from the mill

1 pinch sugar

a few salad leaves to garnish

Keep a few of the best walnut kernels for garnishing, chopping the rest.
Peel and quarter the apples, then remove the core, stalk and flower end. Grate the apple coarsely in a food processor, or cut with a sharp knife into thin strips about 5 mm/¼ inch thick and 3 cm/1¼ inch long.
Mix the apple quickly with the lemon juice in a bowl.
Scrub the celeriac well under cold running water, allow to drain, then quarter and peel. Prepare in the same fashion as the apple, mixing it also in the lemon juice so that it does not discolour.
Beat the cream until stiff, then beat in the mayonnaise, little by little to produce a thick creamy sauce. Season with salt, pepper, and sugar. Mix the

sauce, walnuts, apple and celeriac together. Leave covered in the refrigerator for about 20 minutes to allow all the flavours to mingle, then season again to taste. Garnish four serving dishes with washed, dried salad leaves, heaping the salad on top, and garnishing with the walnut halves. Serve with slices of freshly toasted white bread and a dry sherry (fino).

Preparation time: 25 minutes
Finishing time: (without standing time) 10 minutes

Variations: For especially festive occasions, this salad may be served in hollowed-out apples. In this case, the apple and celeriac must be cut into very small dice. As a garnish, apart from the walnuts, a few cherries and half-orange slices may be used. Waldorf salad tastes especially fruity if some of the apple is replaced by diced fresh pineapple, and the mayonnaise may be replaced by whipped cream, which makes the salad very light. The cream may be refined with some orange liqueur.

Note: Should the flavour of the raw celeriac be found to be too strong, the unpeeled root may be cooked for 10 minutes in lightly-salted boiling water, flavoured with some lemon juice, after which it should be refreshed under cold water, then peeled, before proceeding as above.
Waldorf Salad is one of the best-known starters in international gastronomy. It was presumably created in the Waldorf-Astoria Hotel in New York, whose cooks have "found" many world famous dishes. Waldord Salad may also be piled into peach halves as a garnish for dishes of roast game. It may also be served in poached halves of William pears, and served with cheese, when it should be eaten with a medium-dry oloroso or amontillado sherry.

Onion Salad with Pineapple and Orange

4 large onions

0.125 litres/4 fl oz well-seasoned meat stock

0.005 litres/⅙ fl oz dry white wine

½ fresh pineapple (about 400 grams/14 oz)

4 small oranges (preferably blood oranges)

2 stalks of lemon balm

coarsely ground black pepper

50 grams/1¾ oz mayonnaise

grated rind and juice of 1 untreated lemon

3 tablespoons walnut or grapeseed oil

salt

1 pinch cayenne pepper

1 pinch sugar

Peel the onions and slice very thinly.
Bring the wine and oil to the boil and blanch the onion rings in the mixture for 30 seconds. Remove them with a perforated spoon and plunge into cold water. Allow to drain off and then dry off on kitchen tissue, or spread on a thick layer of kitchen paper to dry.
Peel the pineapple thickly and remove the "eyes" with a small sharp vegetable knife. Cut the pineapple in eight, lengthwise, remove the hard centre and then cut into 5 mm thick slices.
Peel the oranges and remove the white inner membrane. Cut the fruit across into thin slices, removing any pips, if necessary.

Wash the lemon balm, dry, then remove the leaves and cut into thin strips.
Arrange the orange slices onto a serving dish or 4 individual plates, overlapping them like flower petals, and heap the onion rings in the centre. Sprinkle both with pepper, then place the pineapple flesh on the top.
Mix the mayonnaise with the cayenne pepper and oil, flavouring it with salt and pepper and a little sugar, if necessary.
Pour the sauce over the salad but do not mix it in.

Sprinkle with the chopped lemon balm leaves.

This strongly-flavoured fruit salad goes well with game dishes of all kinds. It can also be served with all cold meats or cold roast beef as a main dish.

Preparation time: 25 minutes
Finishing time: 10 minutes

Variations: Originating in the Orient, and well-liked in Italy as a starter or side salad to go with game dishes, here is another variation on the fruit theme. Six small juicy oranges are peeled to the flesh and cut into thin slices, removing pips, if any. Arrange on a serving dish. Chop 1 onion finely as well as some green from spring onions (scallions) and sprinkle over the fruit, together with 100 grams/$3\frac{1}{2}$ oz stoned black olives. Sprinkle the salad with some lemon juice, and a little ground black or white pepper from the mill.

To finish, sprinkle over 3 to 4 tablespoonsful of cold-pressed olive or grapeseed oil. Cover the dish with clingfilm and place in the refrigerator for about 30 minutes before serving.

Christophene Salad with Garlic

The christophene is a small type of marrow originating in Brazil, which can be eaten raw, boiled or stewed.

2 christophenes (each about 400 grams/14 oz)

salt, 1 bayleaf

4 sprigs thyme

2 shallots or small onions

2 cloves garlic

4 tablespoons cold-pressed olive oil (virgin olive oil)

6 tablespoons cream

2 tablespoons herb vinegar

black pepper from mill

1 red and 1 yellow capsicum

½ bunch flat-leaved parsley

If the christophenes are leathery, they should be peeled, otherwise scrub them well under running water, cut them lengthwise into 3, then dice the pieces. Remove any hard inner parts if necessary. Put on a pan to boil containing 1 litre/35 fl oz water together with plenty of salt, bayleaf and thyme and cook the diced christophene for 5 minutes. Remove with a skimmer and allow to drain off and cool. Peel the shallots or onions, then chop them finely. Peel the garlic clove and press it into a paste with some salt. Put the oil into a frying-pan and sweat off the onion and garlic paste without colouring.
Mix in the cream and vinegar and allow to cook to a creamy sauce, then season well with salt and pepper.

Meantime, wash the capsicums, halve them, then remove the seeds and stalk, before cutting them into very small dice. Rinse the parsley, spin it dry then chop finely. Mix the christophenes and capsicums together with the still-warm sauce, and serve immediately. Serve with freshly toasted slices of French bread.

Preparation time: 20 minutes
Finishing time: 10 minutes

<u>Variations:</u> The same method can be used to prepare all types of vegetable marrows, but especially good are courgettes, the white custard marrow and the mild egg marrow.
The custard marrow is so thin-skinned that it need not be peeled, and tastes specially good if it is lightly fried over in butter before use.
Any desired type of marrow can be eaten raw, provided that it is either grated coarsely, or cut into very fine dice first. Instead of the above garlic sauce, herb-flavoured vinaigrette sauce can be used, made from fresh herbs and a clove of garlic puréed in a liquidiser, before mixing with the chosen oil and vinegar. The sauce should be strongly seasoned, as these marrows have little flavour of their own.

Grape and Chestnut Salad

400 grams/14 oz sweet chestnuts

⅛ litre/4 fl oz grape juice

⅛ litre/4 fl oz dry white wine

200 grams/7 oz black dessert grapes

200 grams/7 oz white dessert grapes

⅛ litre/4 fl oz cream

½ teaspoon English mustard powder

1 tablespoon raspberry or sherry vinegar

1 tablespoon walnut or hazelnut oil

1 pinch salt

½ bunch chervil

Cut a cross with a sharp knife at the pointed end of the chestnuts without cutting into the flesh. Place them on a baking sheet in a medium oven at 200°C/400°F (gas mark 6) and roast them until the shells curl outwards. This will take about 20–25 minutes, then peel the chestnuts taking care to remove all of the inner skin. Mix the grape juice and the white wine together and pour over the still warm chestnuts. Leave covered in a cool place for at least 6 hours, preferably overnight, to absorb the flavour. Wash the grapes and dry well.
Remove from the stalks, halve them and remove all the pips. Beat the cream until fairly firm, but not too stiff.

Dissolve the mustard powder in the vinegar. Beat this mixture together with the oil into the cream. Season with salt. Drain off the chestnuts. A little of the liquor may be added to the sauce, if desired. Mix the chestnuts and grapes into the sauce. Rinse and dry the chervil, which can either be left whole, or chopped coarsely. Strew the chervil over the salad. Serve the salad with cocktail rolls and a medium-dry Riesling wine.

Preparation time: (without time for roasting and steeping) 35 minutes
Finishing time: 10 minutes

Variations: The chestnuts and grapes can be moistened with just the wine/grape juice mixture, a little lemon juice, and seasoned with salt and pepper if desired. They can be sprinkled with fresh chives or basil, and a little bowl of soured cream (crème fraîche) may be served with them, so that each diner can prepare his own salad. The grapes can also be mixed with fresh, shelled walnut kernels instead of chestnuts, in which case 200 grams/7 oz will be needed for 4 persons.

Note: For especially festive occasions the grapes can be peeled. This makes for a lot of work, but the final result is well worth the effort, as the flavour is vastly improved. In order to do this with the least effort, stab each grape on to a cocktail stick, plunge it into boiling water, refresh quickly under cold water, and the skins will peel easily with the point of a sharp knife. If seedless grapes can be purchased, the grapes can be left whole, which makes for a more attractive salad. This salad goes very well (in half-quantity) as a side salad with fine game dishes, such as saddle of venison, venison steaks or wild boar fillet.

69

Avocado and Crayfish Salad

2 crayfish (crawfish (U.S.)) tails each about 200 grams/7 oz

$\frac{1}{4}$ litre/8$\frac{1}{2}$ fl oz dry white wine

$\frac{1}{4}$ litre/8$\frac{1}{2}$ fl oz water

$\frac{1}{2}$ untreated lemon

$\frac{1}{2}$ bunch dill

$\frac{1}{2}$ teaspoon green peppercorns

2 untreated limes

2 avocados

1 pink grapefruit

125 grams/4 oz canned lychees

125 grams/4 oz deep-frozen raspberries

4 tablespoons raspberry vinegar

1 tablespoon himbeergeist (raspberry liqueur) (framboise)

1 teaspoon sugar

15 ml/$\frac{1}{2}$ fl oz cream

salt, cayenne pepper

Wash the crayfish tails briefly under running water. Mix the water and wine in a pan. Cut the lemon into slices. rinse and shake-dry the dill. Place all together with the green peppercorns and the crayfish tails into the pan and bring to the boil and simmer together for about 8 minutes. Remove the tails from the liquor with a skimmer, drain them off and remove the flesh from the shells. Scrub one lime under running water, dry it and cut it in slices. Squeeze the juice from the second one. Peel the avocados, halve them length-wise and remove the stone.

Slice the fruit lengthwise and arrange it on a large serving dish in a star shape. Sprinkle the flesh immediately with the lime juice so that it does not discolour. Garnish the avocados with the sliced limes. Peel the grapefruit to the flesh, removing all the white pith. Cut out the fruit in segments without the membrane using a sharp knife, then cut the segments across. Drain the lychees and mix them with the grapefruit. Place this mixture in the middle of the dish. Cut the crayfish flesh into 5 mm/$\frac{1}{4}$ inch thick slices and arrange these around the outside of the dish. Place the defrosted raspberries, raspberry vinegar and liqueur with the sugar and cream into the bowl of a mixer and reduce it into a smooth creamy sauce. Season with the salt and cayenne pepper and pour it over the salad, but do not mix it in. Serve this salad with oven-fresh French bread, salted butter and a dry German sparkling wine (Sekt), or a dry white wine, such as Riesling or Muller-Thurgau.

Preparation time: 25 minutes
Finishing time: 10 minutes

Papaya and Mango Salad

2 turkey escalopes (each about 180 grams/6$\frac{1}{2}$ oz)

salt

white pepper from the mill

20 grams clarified butter

curry powder

1 mango

1 papaya (pawpaw)

1 untreated orange

1 untreated lemon

1 teaspoon herb mustard

1 small carton soured cream (crème fraîche) (100 grams/3$\frac{1}{2}$ oz)

50 grams/1$\frac{3}{4}$ oz coarsely chopped pistachio nuts

coarsely ground mixed pepper

Rub the turkey escalopes with salt, pepper and curry powder. Heat the clarified butter in a frying pan, place in the es-calopes and fry each side for 3 minutes, then allow to cool. Peel the mango, cutting it into 4 segments and peel them from the stone. Remove the flesh from the segments using a sharp knife. Halve the papaya and remove the pips from it with a spoon, quarter the fruit lengthwise, peel it and dice the flesh. Scrub the orange and lime under running water, dry well, and grate the zest from 1 half of the orange. Remove the zest from the lime in thin strips using a zester. Halve the lime and from each half cut 2 thin slices. The halved orange and lime can then be squeezed. Cut the turkey flesh across the grain into thin strips, then mix with the diced papaya. Decorate a flat serving dish with the mango pieces. Scatter the orange peel over the top. Place

the papaya and turkey mixture
in the centre. Mix
together the orange and
lime juice with the mustard
and soured cream and season
with the salt. Pour over the
salad. Scatter the pistachio nuts,
lime zest and as much pepper as
desired. Garnish with the
slices of lime. Serve with
freshly toasted white bread.
Mango does not go well
with wine, so no alcoholic
drink is recommended with
this recipe.

Preparation time: 40 minutes
Finishing time: 10 minutes

Lamb's Lettuce with Poultry Livers

200 grams/7 oz large-leaved lamb's lettuce

the light inner leaves of a head of chicory

300 grams/11 oz fresh poultry livers (chicken, turkey or duck)

15 grams/½ oz butter

white pepper from the mill

1 large pinch mixed herbs (commercial product)

salt

4 cl/14 fl oz dry sherry (fino)

3 tablespoons cream

2 shallots

½ clove garlic

1 small carton soured cream (crème fraîche) (100 grams/3½ oz)

2 tablespoons cold-pressed olive oil (virgin olive oil), or walnut oil

1 tablespoon sherry vinegar

Pick over the lamb's lettuce and wash well several times. Leave to drain in a colander. Wash the chicory, shake dry and tear into bite-sized pieces. Put to one side. Rinse the livers under running water, dab dry with kitchen tissue. Remove all sinews and veins, then cut into bite-sized cubes. Heat the butter in a pan and place the cubed liver in, moving it around so that it does not become too brown. Sprinkle with pepper, mixed herbs and salt. Pour in the sherry and cream, mixing all together so that a light creamy sauce is produced. Season again to taste. In the meantime, peel the shallots and chop finely. Press the garlic clove through a garlic press. Beat the soured cream, oil and sherry vinegar together with a whisk until smooth. Season with salt and pepper to taste. Mix with the shallots and garlic. Split the salad leaves into 4 portions and decorate 4 dishes with it. Pour over the salad dressing. Place the still warm livers and their sauce in the centre. Serve with white French bread and a dry white wine, such as Riesling or Muller-Thurgau, or a light cool rosé.

Preparation time: 30 minutes
Finishing time: 10 minutes

Note: If fresh livers are not obtainable, confidently use deep-frozen. In general, chicken livers are offered in 500 grams/1 lb packs. They are very cheap and tasty, and have next to no waste, yielding over 300 grams per pack. If you wish to add something special to the flavour, after cleaning the livers, leave them to marinade for a good hour in a little port wine, before frying. Make sure that they are dried well before frying.

Variation: Instead of poultry livers, finely sliced calf's liver may be used for the salad, and calf's kidney stewed in sherry cream can also be substituted, but the shallots should be fried off with them and the garlic omitted.

Shrimp Salad in Tomatoes

200 grams/7 oz fresh or deep-frozen North Sea shrimps

4 tablespoons finest quality mayonnaise (or homemade)

3 tablespoons cream

1 tablespoon lemon, or lime juice

1 tablespoon brandy or cognac

1 tablespoon tomato ketchup

salt

white pepper from the mill

1 pinch ground coriander

4 large firm tomatoes

$\frac{1}{2}$ salad cucumber

$\frac{1}{2}$ bunch dill

1 tablespoon herb vinegar

2 tablespoons very good salad oil

Rinse the shrimps briefly under running water (frozen ones must be thawed first). Allow to drain off, then spread them on to a thick layer of kitchen tissue. Mix the mayonnaise with the cream, lemon or lime juice, brandy or cognac and the tomato ketchup and beat well, using a hand whisk, or an electric beater. Season with salt, pepper and coriander. Mix with the shrimps in a bowl, and allow to stand for about 10 minutes. In the meantime, wash and dry the tomatoes. Cut a lid from the top of each. Remove the flesh and pips carefully. This can be done easily with a grapefruit knife. Chop the firm fruit flesh and the lids and put to one side. Fill the shrimp salad mixture into the tomato shells. Peel the half-cucumber, cut in half lengthwise and remove the seeds. Cut again lengthwise,

then cut into cubes. Rinse off the dill and shake dry before chopping. Mix the herb vinegar and oil with a little salt. Mix the tomato dice with the cucumber and the vinegar/oil mixture. Set the tomato shells on to a dish, arranging the cucumber salad around. Garnish the cucumber with the dill. Serve this salad with rounds of buttered black bread and an ice-cold glass of Akvavit or Vodka before a substantial fish dish, or a solid roast.

Preparation time: 20 minutes
Finishing time: 10 minutes

Variation: Do not fill the shrimp salad into tomato shells, but garnished over cooked white asparagus, together with diced skinned tomatoes and a little chopped basil scattered over. The

shrimp salad also tastes very good over very tender 4 cm/2 inch lengths of cooked salsify, mixed with skinned tomato flesh.

75

Guacamole

(Avocado Purée)

Although guacamole originated in Mexico it has also been found in all those countries of central America in which the avocado tree is grown.

The avocado pear is not only especially nourishing, full of vitamins and minerals, but a very valuable fruit. There is no basic recipe for guacamole, and almost every housewife has her own recipe for it. Whether or not guacamole is thought of simply as just as a purée, it has as much justification to be considered in the ranks of salads as the following recipe, "Poor Man's Caviar".

2 small onions
1 large firm preserved green pepper (from jar)
4 small firm-fleshed tomatoes
½ bunch flat-leaved parsley
2 ripe avocados
salt, black pepper from the mill
freshly squeezed lime or lemon juice
a few salad leaves

Peel and chop the onions finely. Drain off the pepper, halve it, remove the seeds and chop it if necessary. Blanch the tomatoes in boiling water, then refresh them in cold water and skin them. Cut them into quarters, remove the seeds and the cores. Cut the flesh into dice. Rinse and shake dry the parsley, keeping one sprig by for garnishing, before chopping the rest. Peel the avocados, halve them lengthwise and remove the stones. Mash the flesh up with a fork. Mix with the above ingredients and season with salt, pepper and lemon juice. Prepare the guacamole as near to the time of service as possible, as avocado flesh will discolour quickly. Serve the guacamole on the salad leaves, garnish with the chopped parsley and serve with French bread or toast. Following Central American or Mexican custom it may also be served with small thin pancakes (tortillas). As a drink, Tequila (agave root brandy) may be served, with a slice of lemon.

Preparation time: 15 minutes
Finishing time: 10 minutes

Variations: If a stronger-flavoured guacamole is desired, replace the green pepper with a fresh red or green chili pepper. Many also add 1–2 sieved hard-boiled eggs to the mixture. A chopped green capsicum and a little oil may also be added. In order to be accurate to its origins, parsley should be replaced by Cilantro (coriander leaves), but this is difficult to find. A similar flavour can be arrived at by using a half-and-half mixture of flat-leaved parsley and chervil.

Poor Man's Caviar
(Aubergine Purée)

This purée is known under the above name in the area around the Capsian Sea. Even here the method of preparation varies a little according to the area and family recipes. The basic recipe originates in Persia.

600 grams/21 oz aubergines	
4 cloves garlic	
1 bunch flat-leaved parsley	
2 small sprigs peppermint	
$\frac{1}{8}$ litre/4 fl oz sunflower oil	
salt, white pepper from the mill	
1 tablespoon lemon juice	
vinegar to taste	
1 sprig lovage	

Prick the aubergines several times with a fork and put into a pre-heated oven at 250°C/500°F (gas mark 9) and roast for about 25 minutes, until the skin is crinkled and bubbly. Refresh the aubergines under cold water, remove the skin, and press out the moisture either with the hands or using a sieve. Chop the flesh very fine, or purée it in a mixer. Peel the garlic. Rinse and dry the peppermint and the parsley. The garlic can either be put into the mixer or pressed in a garlic press first, then added to the mixture. The peppermint and the parsley should be chopped finely before adding to the aubergine mixture. Add the oil slowly, as for making mayonnaise, while beating and season the "caviar" with salt, pepper, lemon juice and vinegar. Fill it into a bowl and decorate with the previously washed and dried lovage. Serve with black olives and a light country-style bread.

Preparation time: (without time for "baking") 15 minutes
Finishing time: (5 minutes using a food processor, otherwise) 10 minutes

Variations: 1 green and red capsicum can be added to the recipe (prepared as on page 48). Parsley may be substituted by fresh basil, in which case the purée will not need additional pepper for seasoning.

77

Bagna Cauda

(Italian Vegetable Fondue)

Bagna Cauda could be called just a "hot sauce", but what a sauce! It must be fragrant with garlic and be rich in anchovies. The rest of the contents will vary from one valley in Piedmont to the next, where this dish originates, as well as the vegetable mixture which accompanies it. This all depends on what the market offers. The quantity will also vary, depending on whether it is intended as a starter or a main dish. The range of vegetables is endless. For example, carrots cut in strips, strips of red and green capsicums, cucumber, cardoons (a type of edible thistle, related to the artichoke), celery, slices of mushroom, blanched cauliflower florets, canned artichoke hearts or bottoms, palm hearts, and even fresh shelled walnuts.

Simple Garlic and Anchovy Sauce

100 grams/3½ oz bottled or canned anchovy fillets
6 cloves garlic
50 grams/2 oz butter
¼ litre/9 fl oz cold-pressed olive oil (virgin olive oil)

Rinse the anchovy fillets under running water and dry on kitchen tissue.
Put them into a mortar and mix to a paste, or chop them very finely.
Peel the garlic and chop just as finely.
Put the butter into an earthenware heatproof pan (normally used for this dish) and heat. Add the garlic and stew it until very soft, then add the oil gradually, and finally add the anchovy paste. Let it cook gently for about 10 minutes, without letting the oil get too hot. Stir from time to time. Bring the pot to the table and keep it hot on a rechaud (plate warmer). Serve the prepared vegetables with it. Each guest chooses vegetables according to taste and dips them into the hot sauce. Serve this dish with fresh French bread and a light dry white wine, such as a young Barbera.

Preparation time: (without time to clean the vegetables) 15 minutes
Finishing time: 15 minutes

Bagna Cauda with Sour Cream

Prepare the basic sauce as above, using 75 grams/3 oz butter but only ⅛ litre/4½ fl oz of oil. Add to this ⅛ litre/4½ fl oz of soured cream, or better still crème fraîche beaten in. Once the cream has been added, do not allow the sauce to boil.
This sauce acquires a special note if 25–30 grams/¾–1 oz sliced white truffle is added (canned black truffle can also be used).

Note: This sauce tastes extra good as a dip for cooked artichokes.

78

Bagna Cauda with Cream

Prepare the anchovy fillets and garlic as described above, but using only 6 anchovy fillets and 4 cloves of garlic. From $\frac{3}{8}$ litre/13 fl oz cream beat half and add the other half to the above mixture. In another pan heat 100 grams/3$\frac{1}{2}$ oz butter, add the anchovy fillets and the garlic paste and allow to cook gently for 10 minutes, stirring all the time. Add the thickened cream a spoonful at a time, beating it strongly all the time with a whisk. The finished sauce should not be cooked further.

Advice: For the basic sauce there two other easy, but very delicate variations.
Firstly, the finished sauce can be refined with 4 tablespoons of cream, or secondly, 6 cl/2 fl oz full-bodied red wine together with 1–2 tea-spoonfuls of white breadcrumbs could be added.

Salsify Salad with King Prawns

Salsify, the "asparagus of winter" is available fresh in the market between October and March. Its delicate nutty flavour makes it so desirable to conoisseurs.

King prawns may also be known as scampi or giant prawns, depending on their source.

250 grams/9 oz king prawns

500 grams/18 oz salsify

4 tablespoons vinegar

½ litre/18 fl oz water, salt

10 grams/⅓ oz butter

1 teaspoon lemon juice

100 grams/3½ oz watercress

1 young carrot

1 small carton soured cream (crème fraîche)

4 tablespoons cream

2 tablespoons sherry vinegar

cayenne pepper

Worcestershire sauce

1 bunch dill

2 tablespoons walnut oil

Thaw out the king prawns according to the instructions on the packet.

Scrub the salsify under running water. It is best to do this wearing rubber gloves, as the peel has juices which run out and are extremely difficult to remove from the hands. Prepare a basin with vinegar/water mixture. Peel the salsify thinly, but completely with an asparagus peeler, then cut into 6 cm/2½ inch lengths, and put each length immediately into the vinegar/water mixture, in order that the salsify does not become discoloured. When all the salsify is peeled and cut, bring a pan to the boil with water, salt, butter and lemon juice. Put in the salsify and cook it covered with a lid for about 15–20 minutes until cooked but still firm.

In the meantime, clean the watercress and wash well, then leave it to drain in a colander, shaking off as much water as possible. Peel the carrot and

grate coarsely. Mix the soured cream with the cream and sherry vinegar into a smooth sauce, and season with the cayenne pepper, Worcestershire sauce, and a little salt. Wash off the dill, dab it dry, cut it up finely, and add it to the sauce.

Drain the salsify and allow to cool a little. It should be served while still a little warm. The king prawns should be briefly rinsed, allowed to drain, and laid on a layer of household tissue, dabbed dry. Four individual dishes should be decorated with the watercress, sprinkled with the walnut oil, and the carrot scattered on top. The salsify should be

arranged in a star fashion on top, and the king prawn dressed in a heap on top. The dill sauce should be poured over, and the salad served immediately. Serve it with a dry white wine.

Preparation time: (without defrosting time) 50 minutes
Finishing time: 15 minutes

Variation: Pacific prawns, a type of scampi can be used in this recipe, instead of king

prawns. They originate in the South Pacific, off Chile and are caught, cooked and deep-frozen there, being exported to Europe. Their red-white marbled flesh is very tasty and tender.

81

Warm Fennel and Mushroom Salad

3 small bulbs of fennel

3 sticks of celery

125 grams/4½ oz shallots

¼ stick leek

5 fresh or dried sprigs thyme

¼ teaspoon coriander seeds

1 clove garlic

1 bayleaf

⅛ litre/4 fl oz water

juice of 1 large lemon

6 tablespoons cold-pressed olive oil (virgin olive oil)

salt

300 grams/11 oz white button mushrooms

2 tomatoes

1 bunch flat-leaved parsley

black pepper from the mill

Clean off the fennel bulbs and celery, cutting off the leaves, washing and leaving to drain. Cut the fennel lengthwise into 6 or 8. Cut the celery sticks into 5 cm/2 inch lengths. Peel the shallots. Make up a faggot (bouquet garni).

Cut up the leek lengthwise, wash thoroughly and allow to drain.

Take one of the leek leaves, placing in it the fennel and celery leaves, the thyme, the coriander seeds, the peeled garlic clove, and tie the whole together.

Put a large pan on to heat containing the water, with the lemon juice, oil and the faggot (bouquet garni) and bring to the boil, with plenty of salt. Put in the celery and fennel and let it simmer for about 5 minutes.

In the meantime, free the mushrooms from their stalks and rub them over with a clean kitchen cloth. Wash them, only if necessary, and allow to dry well, before adding them to the pan, after which allow them to cook for a further 5 minutes.

Remove the vegetables and the faggot from the pan. Reduce the cooking liquor by half over full heat. Season with salt and some lemon juice, if necessary.

Blanch the tomatoes in boiling water, then refresh and skin them, cutting them in quarters and remove the seeds and core. Cut the fruit into dice.

Rinse the parsley, dab dry and chop. Place the vegetables on to a serving dish, or 4 plates, pour over the liquor, scatter over the tomato dice and parsley and serve while still warm. Grind some black pepper over, if desired.

Serve with fresh country bread and a strong dry, white wine from Spain or Italy.

Preparation time: 40 minutes
Finishing time: 10 minutes

Variations: Apart from the mushrooms, most vegetables are interchangeable in this recipe, such as florets of cauliflower, spring onions, tender leeks (only the tender lower parts), fresh artichoke bottoms, young carrots, or young celeriac.

Note: For the faggot always take a 15 cm/6 inch length of leek cut out from that part of the vegetable where the light green leaves change into dark green and they begin to open out.

Tomato and Mozzarella Salad

This dish which originates in southern Italy is also served there in the summer months as a main dish. It is usually served elsewhere as a starter. Mozzarella is a cheese speciality which originated in the Campania region but is now sold everywhere, usually vacuum packed in brine, and mainly made from cow's milk. In its native area, loose Mozzarella may be purchased, made from the original buffalo's milk, which has a hearty flavour and a slightly yellow colour.

750 grams/26 oz beef-steak tomatoes (not too large)	
250 grams/9 oz Mozzarella cheese	
salt, black pepper from the mill	
3 tablespoons very good vinegar (preferably aceto balsamico)	
1 bunch large-leaved basil	
cold-pressed olive oil (virgin olive oil)	

84

Wash and dry the tomatoes, cutting them into 5 mm/¼ inch thick slices.
Alternate the tomato and cheese slices on a dish, or individual serving plates. Season with salt and pepper and sprinkle the vinegar over. Rinse and dry the basil, then tear up and slice thinly. Scatter over the salad.
Prepare the oil in a flask, so that each diner can help himself as desired.
This salad should be served with fresh French bread and a cool rosé wine.

Preparation time: 10 minutes
Finishing time: 5 minutes

Variations: Cucumber slices may be added to the salad. Green, stoned olives may be added to the salad if wished. Green and red capsicums (prepared as on page 48) cut into 2 cm/1 inch strips may also be added to the salad. In this case add also 1–2 spring onions, where the green part is cut across into rings, and the white part chopped.

Spring Onion Salad

2 large bunches spring onions
8 cl/3 fl oz dry white wine
4 tablespoons wine vinegar
4 tablespoons cold-pressed olive oil (virgin olive oil)
4 stalks parsley
4 stalks fresh thyme, or alternatively 2 stalks dried thyme
6 stalks or 8 large leaves of fresh basil
1 hard-boiled egg
1 tablespoon ground hazelnuts
1 small carton soured cream (crème fraîche) (100 grams/$3\frac{1}{2}$ oz)

Clean the spring onions. Cut off the white bulbs and put to one side.
From the green part, remove only the hard tips, then cut them all into the same length. Make up 4 bunches of the green parts and tie with thread.
Put $\frac{1}{4}$ litre/9 fl oz water into a pan, together with the wine, vinegar, and oil. Salt well and bring to the boil.

In the meantime, wash the parsley and thyme and dry it well. Put the spring onion green, parsley and thyme into the pan. Cook the green for 5 minutes so that it is still firm to the bite (al dente). Remove it with a skimmer and allow to drain then lay it on a thick layer of kitchen tissue. Pour the cooking liquor through a hair sieve and allow to cool. Rinse the basil, dry, and chop it into fine strips. Shell the egg and chop finely. Chop the white of the spring onions also. Place the ground hazelnuts into a non-stick pan and fry until golden brown, without using any fat.
Beat the soured cream with a whisk until light and frothy, then add the cooking liquor little by little. Season the resulting sauce as desired, with a little vinegar and salt.

Cut free the bundles of spring onion green and place on a serving dish, or individual serving plates. Put on the sauce, then scatter first the chopped onion and egg, then the basil and hazelnuts.

This salad goes well with a nut bread and salted butter, and a light, but dry white wine.

Note: After cleaning, spring onions should not need further washing, but if they are grown in the open air, they may need a wash which is best done in a bowl with plenty of water and they should then be shaken dry several times.

Variation: Instead of using the above sauce, spring onions can be served in a strong vinaigrette (see page 29) with capers and herbs. If spring onions are unavailable, young tender leeks may be substituted. Remove the root end before cooking and cut to an even size, removing any hard upper leaves beforehand, preferably just where they change colour from light to dark green. The tender green leafy part should be cut across with a sharp knife. The leeks should be cooked as above, but a further 2 minutes should be added. Leek salad tastes especially good as a starter before a substantial roast, or it can be served as an accompaniment.

87

Duck Breast on Batavia Salad

2 duck breasts (each about
200 grams/7 oz)

salt

white pepper from mill

1 pinch ground sage

10 grams/$\frac{1}{3}$ oz butter

1 batavia lettuce

2 small spring onions

2 bottled ginger plums

1 teaspoon ginger syrup

3 tablespoons raspberry
vinegar

2 tablespoons walnut or
grapeseed oil

3 tablespoons cream

20 grams/$\frac{2}{3}$ oz walnut kernels

Rinse and dry the duck breasts.
Rub in with salt, pepper and
sage. Melt the butter and
brush the bottom of a flat
casserole with it.
Lay in the duck breasts skin-
side uppermost and place the
casserole in a pre-heated oven
at 250°C/500°F (gas mark 9).
Cook for 12–15 minutes. The
breasts should still be a light
pink colour.

Remove them from the
casserole and allow to drain
off. Dab them off with kitchen
tissue and wrap them quickly
singly in aluminium foil
keeping them for later use.
Allow to cool down, but not
below lukewarm.
Pull the batavia to pieces,
wash the leaves and shake
them dry.
Clean the spring onions, chopping the white and cutting the
green into thin rings.
Chop the ginger plums and
put to one side. Mix the
ginger syrup, vinegar, oil and
cream together into a smooth
sauce, and season with the salt
and pepper. Chop the walnut
kernels and add to the sauce.
Arrange the salad leaves in a
star shape on a dish, or 4
portion plates and sprinkle
with the dressing. Scatter the
spring onion on top.
Unwrap the duck breasts, and
if necessary dab them dry
again. Remove the skin. If
there is a layer of fat beneath
the skin, it should be removed.
Then cut the duck breasts
thinly against the grain and
arrange on the salad in a petal
shape. Scatter the chopped
ginger over the top.
Cut the skin in very fine strips
and place in the centre of the
salad.
Serve at once.

This salad goes well with
ovenfresh French bread and a
cool rosé wine.

Preparation time: 35 minutes
Finishing time: 15 minutes

Variations: The duck breasts
can be replaced with roasted
chicken breasts, in which case
the skin must be removed, and
the tender spring onions may
be replaced with sweet
pickled silverskin onions or
shallots. The salad also tastes
good made with slices of
saddle of hare, or venison
(leftovers can be made use of).

Note: Except from a specialist
poulterer, duck breasts can
seldom be obtained on their
own; a whole duck must be
purchased. In this case, roast
the whole duck for about
20 minutes, then remove from
the oven, and take off the
breasts for the salad. Remove
also the legs and remaining
flesh. Chop up the carcase and
together with a chopped onion
and root vegetables return to
the oven. Using water and red
wine, an excellent basic sauce
can be made. From this, with
the rest of the duck flesh, a
very good stew can be
prepared for the next day.

Lettuce Hearts with Egg-Yolk Cream and Matjes Herring

2 large tight green lettuces
4 tender Matjes herring fillets in oil (each about 60 grams/2 oz)
2 hard-boiled eggs
2 raw egg yolks
1 teaspoon English mustard powder
3 tablespoons herb vinegar
3 tablespoons walnut or grapeseed oil
2 tablespoons sour cream
salt
2 small shallots
½ bunch dill
½ bunch flat-leaved parsley
a few radishes, and some chives for garnishing

Remove the outer leaves from the lettuce, so that only the tender green leaves remain. Quarter the heads of lettuce, and wash carefully, then shake them as dry as possible, before putting them to one side. Dry the herring fillets carefully with kitchen tissue, then remove as many bones as possible, using a pair of tweezers, if necessary. Then cut the fillets against the grain into as thin slices as possible, using a smoked-salmon knife if available.

Shell the hard-boiled eggs and remove the yolk. Chop the whites finely, then press the yolks through a sieve. Mix together the raw egg yolks, mustard powder, vinegar and oil in a mixer into a smooth sauce. Finally add the sour cream, and season with the salt. Peel the shallots and chop finely. Rinse the dill and parsley and shake dry. Keep back a few sprigs of the dill for garnishing. Cut up the rest finely, and add, with the chopped parsley, to the sauce. Clean the radishes, and cut into roses. Rinse the chives, dry off and chop them into little rings. Garnish each salad plate with a quarter of a lettuce and pour over a little of the sauce. Arrange the herring fillet slices on the plate overlapping, like roof tiles, then sprinkle with the remaining sauce. Scatter the shallots and

chopped egg over the lettuce hearts. Garnish the herring fillets with the sprigs of dill, radish roses, and chopped chives.

Serve the salad with lightly buttered blackbread slices or circles of pumpernickel, and a dry white wine, or ice-cold aquavit.

Variations: This salad can be enriched by replacing the herring fillets with smoked salmon. The lettuce can also be cut into eighths and arranged star-fashion on the plate, with a poached egg placed in the centre. This can have the sauce dressed over it and be garnished with smoked salmon slices.

Note: Matjes herring in oil are usually so tender that they need no rinsing, but should be tasted to see if they are too salty. If that is the case, they should be placed in a half and half mixture of buttermilk and mineral water, or weak black tea for 30 minutes, before use.

Salade Nicoise

Salade Nicoise has long been found well outside the area of the French district of Provence, but will always contain the basic ingredients, lettuce, tuna fish, tomatoes and herbs, although others may be added. This recipe is a refined variation of the original which is frequently served as a starter, in Provence.

100 grams/3½ oz Kenya, or Princess beans

salt

1 small head of lettuce or chicory

1 each green and red capsicum

2–3 stalks of celery

4–5 fleshy, firm tomatoes

1 can tuna fish in oil (200 grams/3½ oz)

16 black olives

1 large white onion

½ bunch flat-leaved parsley

5 sprigs fresh basil

5 tablespoons cold-pressed olive oil (virgin olive oil)

4 tablespoons wine vinegar

salt, black pepper from mill

2 hard-boiled eggs

Prepare the beans and put to cook in a pan of well-salted water for about 8 minutes. They should still be crisp. Drain off and allow to cool. Clean the lettuce or chicory, wash the leaves, shake well dry, then tear into pieces. Remove any hard centre stalks. Wash the capsicums, quarter them, remove the core and seeds, and cut across into thin strips.
Clean the celery sticks, wash, drain, then cut up lengthwise. Cut the sticks across into 2 cm/¾ inch slices.
Wash dry and cut the tomatoes in eighths, removing the core and stalk.
Drain off the tuna fish, but keep the oil from the can. Break the fish up into bite-sized pieces.

Halve the olives, removing the stones, if necessary.
Peel the onion and cut into thin rings.
Rinse and dry the parsley and basil and chop coarsely.
Make up a sauce from the olive oil, vinegar, salt, pepper, and as much of the liquor from the tuna as desired.
Lay the lettuce into a large bowl. Mix together the other salad ingredients and put into the bowl. Pour over the sauce.
Shell the eggs and cut into eighths. Garnish the salad with them.
Serve the salad with French sticks and a light red vin de pays, if possible.

Preparation time: 25 minutes
Finishing time: 10 minutes

Variations: This salad can be made using rinsed rolled anchovy fillets as a garnish. In this case, do not over-salt the sauce. Alternatively, no sauce is made for the salad, but salt, peppermill, oil and vinegar is placed on the table, so that each diner can dress his salad according to taste.

93

Curly Endive Salad with Garlic Croutons

1 large head curly endive

100 grams/3½ oz de-fatted raw ham

1 bunch mixed seasonal herbs

2 shallots

2 hard-boiled eggs

2 large fresh cloves of garlic

20 grams/⅔ oz butter

3 slices not-too-fresh white bread

1 teaspoon strong mustard

3 tablespoons red wine vinegar

6 tablespoons oil

salt

50 grams/1¾ oz chopped walnut kernels

coarsely-ground black pepper

Clean and tear apart the endive, then wash and allow to drain in a colander.
Cut the ham into dice or fine strips.
Rinse, shake dry and chop the herbs.
Peel the shallots, then cut into rings, or chop finely.
Shell the eggs, then cut in halves. Separate whites from yolks. Chop the whites into dice and keep the yolks until later.

Peel the cloves of garlic, then pass them through a garlic press, or press into a paste with the blade of a knife. Heat the butter in a large pan and skim the curd from the butter. Put in the garlic and let it sweat off until glazed, turning occasionally, then remove from pan. Trim the crusts from the bread and cut into 1 cm/½ inch cubes. Fry these off in the butter until golden brown. Keep warm. Press the egg yolk through a sieve and mix it with the mustard and vinegar. Add the oil, drop by drop until a light, creamy sauce is produced. Season with salt. Tear up the endive leaves into bite-sized pieces, then mix with the ham, herbs, shallots and egg whites. Mix with the sauce and place into a serving dish. Scatter the top with the garlic croutons and the chopped walnuts. Sprinkle with pepper if desired.

This salad tastes very good as a starter with a substantial meat dish, such as roast game, or saddle of lamb.

Preparation time: 25 minutes
Finishing time: 10 minutes

Variation: This salad can also be prepared using an open-air grown lettuce, or large-leaved Lamb's lettuce.

Note: When looking for garlic, remember that only the freshest is good enough. Not only are the flavour and aroma at their best, but there will be less "after odour". If old cloves are to be used, remove the inner heart and only use the outside part of the clove. If the clove of garlic is a brown colour, throw it away.

Salad with Oyster Mushrooms

Oyster mushrooms normally grow in Autumn and Winter on the living and dead stumps of deciduous trees. These extremely tasty wild mushrooms were once seen only seldom on the market, but are now being cultivated, and notwithstanding this, are still difficult to obtain, if compared with the cultivated mushroom. Besides its aromatic flavour, it has a very firm flesh, which gives it its other name, that of "veal mushroom". If the quantity produced were to be increased, it would be a fierce rival to the ordinary mushroom.

Ingredients
250 grams/9 oz pork fillet (tenderloin) (from the thick end)
1 clove garlic
8 tablespoons thistle or grapeseed oil
salt
500 grams/18 oz oyster mushrooms
1 small onion
1 bunch parsley
white pepper from mill
6 tablespoons cream
100 grams/3½ oz lamb's lettuce
2 small heads radicchio
2 tablespoons sherry vinegar
1 tablespoon medium dry sherry
½ teaspoon English mustard powder
1 pinch sugar
coarsely ground green or mixed peppers

Skin the pork fillet if necessary, then rub dry with a kitchen tissue, and rub all over with the peeled and halved garlic clove.

Heat 2 tablespoons oil in a pan, and fry the fillet over a medium heat for about 15—20 minutes. Leave to drain, salt all over, then wrap it in aluminium foil. Put it to one side to keep warm. It will lose heat slowly in the foil. Meantime, clean the mushrooms well. If possible, do not wash them, but rub them in a kitchen cloth. Cut large ones in halves or quarters. In the pan in which the meat was cooked, add a further 2 tablespoons of oil, put in the mushrooms and fry for about 10 minutes, turning them frequently. Peel the onion, rinse off the parsley and dab it dry. Chop both and after 5 minutes add to the mush-

rooms. Season with salt and pepper. Pour in the cream, stirring all the time, and cook for a further 3 minutes without allowing to boil.

Clean the lamb's lettuce well, wash and allow to drain. Pull the radicchio to pieces, wash well and allow to drain, then cut into bite-sized pieces. Decorate a serving dish with the radicchio and lamb's lettuce. Mix the sherry vinegar, sherry and mustard powder together, season with salt and pepper, then finally mix in the rest of the oil. Sprinkle the salad with this mixture. Heap the mushrooms on top. Unwrap the fillet and cut into very thin slices, arranging it in a petal shape on top of the mushrooms. Scatter the ground pepper over the top and serve immediately.

This salad only needs fresh white bread and a dry white wine (Riesling) or a dry sherry (fino) to make a good meal.

Preparation time:
35 minutes
Finishing time:
10 minutes

Variation: Instead of oyster mushrooms, cèpes (Fr.) (boletus edulis) may be used, in which case they only need 5 minutes frying at the most.

97

Mushroom Salad
with Tomato Parfait

¼ litre/9 fl oz pure tomato juice

4 juniper berries

6 peppercorns

1 teaspoon bottled grated horseradish

6 sprigs parsley

3 sheets white gelatine

salt

1 pinch sugar

1 cl/⅓ fl oz gin

25 grams/1 oz ground hazelnuts

1 carton cream yoghurt

1 egg yolk

2 tablespoons walnut oil

2 tablespoons cream

black pepper from mill

125 grams/4 oz large-leaved lamb's lettuce

200 grams/3½ oz large white mushrooms

1 tablespoon lemon juice

1 bunch chives

Put the tomato juice into a saucepan. Grind the juniper berries and peppercorns in a mortar, adding them and the horseradish to the juice in the pan. Put in the rinsed, dried parsley into the pan and gradually bring it to the boil. Roll up the gelatine and soak it in cold water. Take the pan from the heat and dissolve the pressed-out gelatine in the juice. Pour the juice from the pan through a sieve and flavour it with the salt, sugar and gin. Fill it into a mould and let it set for about 2 hours in a refrigerator.
For the sauce, fry off the ground hazelnuts in a non-stick pan without fat, stirring continuously until golden brown. Place the yoghurt and egg yolk in a mixer and beat, adding the oil and cream a little at a time. Add the nuts and season with salt and pepper.

Clean the lamb's lettuce well, wash it and allow to drain in a colander, or pat it dry in a kitchen towel.
Clean the mushrooms, washing only if necessary, and drying thoroughly if washed. Cut them into slices, but not too thin, placing them immediately into lemon juice. Rinse and dry the chives, then cut them into little rolls and

add them to the sauce.
Dip the mould with the
tomato parfait momentarily
into hot water, turn out the
parfait and cut it into small
cubes. Decorate individual
plates with the lamb's lettuce.
Sprinkle it with the sauce.
Arrange the mushroom slices
on top petal fashion, pouring
over the rest of the sauce.
Scatter the tomato parfait

cubes over the top of the
salad, and serve immediately.

This salad will go well with
any puff pastry items and a
light dry white wine.

Preparation time: (without
setting time) 35 minutes
Finishing time: 10 minutes

Variations: Instead of white
mushrooms, this salad can be
made using oyster mushrooms
or cèpes (boletus edulis). Both
of these must be fried off first
in butter. Small oyster mushrooms may be left whole, and
the cèpes can be cut into thin
slices. Even slices can be obtained if an egg slicer is used.

**Truffle Salad
in the
Toulouse style**

Italia Pasta Salad

The Great Salad Buffet

Buffets are hard work. Often harder than a menu with many courses, but they permit many guests to be invited, in this case, at least 20 people. Should the number increase, most of the salads in this book are suitable for buffets, except those which must be freshly made, and even these are quickly put together. Fruit salads make the perfect sweet ending to a meal.

Celery and
Cheese Salad

Mushroom and
Avocado Salad

Truffle Salad in the Toulouse Style

5 hard-boiled eggs

1 teaspoon strong mustard (Dijon, Dusseldorf, or English mustard)

4 tablespoons sherry vinegar

4 tablespoons dry sherry (fino)

salt, white pepper from the mill

1 pinch sugar

8 tablespoons cold-pressed olive oil (virgin olive oil)

16 large artichoke bottoms (bottled or canned)

2 small tins truffles (each about 25 grams/1 oz)

2 large heads Batavia salad

Shell the eggs, cut in halves and remove the yolks. Pass all the yolks and the whites of 2 eggs through a sieve and mix to a smooth paste with the sherry vinegar, sherry, salt, pepper and sugar. Beat in the oil little by little, so that a mayonnaise-like sauce is produced. Drain the artichoke bottoms, then quarter them and cut them into thin strips. Drain off the truffles, and use some of the truffle liquor to flavour the sauce, if desired.

Cut the truffles into very delicate slices. Clean the batavia, pulling it apart. Wash the leaves well, then shake dry. Tear the leaves into bite-sized pieces removing any hard stalks. Cut the remaining egg white into small dice.
Lay out half the salad leaves into a shallow dish. Place on top a third of the artichoke strips and truffle slices. Spread the rest of the salad leaves on top. Arrange the rest of the artichoke strips and truffle slices around so that a space is left in the centre. Place the sauce in this space, and scatter the egg white dice on top. Only mix the salad together just before it is required to be eaten.

Preparation time: 20 minutes
Finishing time: 10 minutes

Italia Pasta Salad

250 grams/9 oz carrots

salt

sugar

500 grams/18 oz multi-coloured pasta bows

1 tablespoon oil

1 pack deep-frozen petits pois (small green peas)

250 grams/9 oz cooked shoulder ham

250 grams/9 oz genuine mortadella sausage

1 bunch spring onions

6 beef tomatoes

6 stalks celery

2 small heads fennel

2 bunches mixed seasonal herbs (or 3 packets deep-frozen mixed herbs)

3 tablespoons capers

250 grams/9 oz finest quality mayonnaise

1 carton soured cream (crème fraîche) (200 grams/7 oz)

10 cl/3½ fl oz cream

cayenne pepper

200 grams/7 oz freshly grated Parmesan cheese

Peel the carrots, and put them to cook gently in a closed pan with a little water and the salt and sugar.
Put 3 litres/106 fl oz water with plenty of salt on to boil, then put in the pasta and cook for about 15 minutes until just cooked (al dente).
Cook the peas at the same time, according to the instructions on the packet.
Turn out the pasta into a colander, refresh under plenty of cold running water and allow to drain well.
Cool the carrots and peas in the same way.
While the pasta is cooking cut the ham and mortadella into small dice.
Clean the spring onions. Chop the white part and cut the green part into thin rings. Blanch the tomatoes, refresh, then skin them and quarter them, removing the seeds and cores. Cut the flesh into dice.
Clean the celery and fennel, wash the leaves and allow to drain.
Cut the celery into thin little strips and the fennel into small dice.
Rinse off the herbs, shake dry and chop them together with the leaves from the celery and fennel. (Allow deep-frozen herbs to thaw first.)
Cut the carrots into slices using a decorating knife.
Allow the capers to drain off.

Mix all ingredients together in a large bowl. Mix the mayonnaise and soured cream together into a smooth sauce and season with salt and cayenne pepper. Mix into the salad ingredients. Allow the salad to stand for 20 minutes before serving, then season again with salt and cayenne pepper.

Put the salad into a serving dish, and the cheese into a small bowl so as to allow guests to sprinkle it over their own salad.

Grape Salad with Roquefort Dressing

500 grams/18 oz black grapes
500 grams/18 oz white grapes
6 stalks celery
4 comice pears
2 sharp apples (Jonathan)

3 tablespoons lemon juice
150 grams/5 oz lamb's lettuce
150 grams/5 oz Roquefort cheese
1 carton soured cream (crème fraîche) (200 grams/7 oz)
4 tablespoons cream
4 tablespoons sherry vinegar
3 tablespoons medium dry sherry (Amontillado)
salt, black pepper from the mill
3 tablespoons walnut or grapeseed oil
50 grams/2 oz walnut kernels

Wash the grapes and allow to drain off.
Pull the grapes from the stalks, cut in halves and remove the pips.
Clean the celery. Wash and dry the leaves. Cut the stalks into very thin slices, and chop the leaves roughly.
Quarter the washed apples and pears, then core, remove stalks and cut into fine dice. Mix quickly with the lemon juice.

Clean the lamb's lettuce, wash well and spin-dry. Cut the Roquefort into coarse cubes, and put it with the soured cream, cream, 2 tablespoons sherry vinegar, sherry, into a mixer and beat into a smooth sauce. Season with the salt and pepper.
Mix the grapes, celery, pears and apples into the sauce. Dress a salad bowl with the lamb's lettuce and sprinkle this with the remaining sherry vinegar and walnut oil. Then heap the salad on the top. Garnish with the walnut kernels.

Preparation time: 40 minutes
Finishing time: 10 minutes

Mushroom and Avocado Salad

200 grams/7 oz lachsschinken (rolled smoked fillet of pork) cut into 5 mm/$\frac{1}{4}$ inch slices
6 shallots
$\frac{1}{8}$ litre/4 fl oz freshly-squeezed lemon juice
600 grams/21 oz cèpes (boletus edulis) mushrooms, or pink mushrooms
4 large avocados
2 teaspoons coriander seeds
6 tablespoons raspberry vinegar or sherry vinegar
$\frac{1}{4}$ teaspoon salt
$\frac{1}{2}$ teaspoon sugar
12 tablespoons walnut or almond oil
coarsely-ground black pepper

Remove the fat from the pork fillet, then cut the flesh into dice.

Peel the shallots and chop finely. Put the lemon juice into a bowl.

Clean the mushrooms one after the other, cut into thin slices and mix straight away with the lemon juice, so that they do not discolour.

Halve the avocados and remove the stones. Cut the flesh out from the skin with a small ball-cutter. Mix the avocado balls and the pork dice together. Grind the coriander seeds coarsely in a mortar, and mix in a bowl with the vinegar, salt and sugar until the sugar has dissolved, then beat continually with a whisk while gradually adding 8 tablespoons of oil to produce a smooth sauce.

Drain the mushrooms and dry off on kitchen tissue if necessary.

The slices should be dressed on to a serving dish over-lapping like roof tiles and sprinkled with the rest of the oil. Scatter with the coriander.

Put the avocado balls and pork dice in the middle and pour over the sauce. Sprinkle with pepper if desired.

Preparation time: 40 minutes
Finishing time: 10 minutes

Note: Large mushrooms can be sliced with an egg slicer which will save time and produce slices of even thickness.

Copenhagen Herring Salad

12 Matjes herring fillets (each about 80 grams/$2\frac{3}{4}$ oz)
1 litre/35 fl oz mineral water
1 small white cabbage (about 750 grams/26 oz)
1 tablespoon salt
1 tablespoon caraway seeds
1 tablespoon peppercorns
4 sharp apples (e.g. Boskop, Granny Smith)
6 red onions
$\frac{1}{4}$ litre/9 fl oz sour cream
$\frac{1}{4}$ litre/9 fl oz cream
6 tablespoons red wine vinegar
black pepper from the mill
300 grams/11 oz streaky (belly) bacon

Only if the herring fillets are very salty should they be left to soak in the mineral water for about 30 minutes. If not, just rinse and dab dry.

Remove any bones, using tweezers, if necessary.

While the fillets are soaking, clean the cabbage, and shred it finely.

Bring a large pan filled with plenty of salted water to the boil. Put the caraway seeds and peppercorns into a gauze bag and tie the top, then place it into the pan. When the water is boiling fast, add the cabbage, allowing it to cook for 3 minutes, then pour out into a colander, refresh with cold water and allow to drain, pressing out as much water as possible.

Quarter, peel, remove core and stalk of the washed apples, and cut into large cubes.

Peel the onions and cut into thin slices. Mix the cream and soured cream with the vinegar. Season well with pepper.

Cut the drained herring fillets against the grain into strips about 1 cm/$\frac{1}{2}$ inch wide.

Put all into a large bowl and mix with the sauce.

Cut the bacon into fine dice and put into a frying pan over a medium heat and fry off slowly. Discard about half of the resulting bacon fat.

Put the salad into a serving dish and pour over the fried bacon.

Preparation time: (without soaking time) 40 minutes
Finishing time: 20 minutes

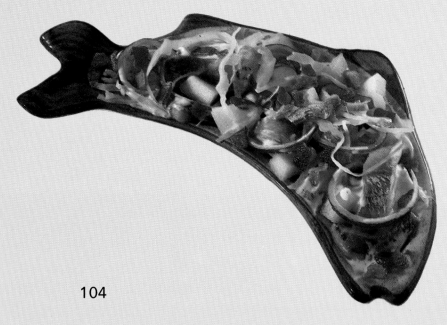

Celery and Cheese Salad

2 heads celery
1 bunch radishes
6 small firm tomatoes
6 shallots
2 cloves garlic
12 Spanish green olives stuffed with pimentoes
50 grams/2 oz butter
450 grams/16 oz white sheep's milk cheese
$\frac{1}{4}$ litre/9 fl oz cream
black pepper from the mill

Clean the celery, pulling off the individual sticks. Cut off the fine tender leaves, wash and dry them and keep to one side. Clean the radishes, wash and dry them, then cut into fine slices.
Blanch the tomatoes with boiling water, refresh and skin them, then cut them into quarters, removing seeds, cores and stalks. Cut the flesh into dice.
Peel the shallots and garlic. Chop the shallots and press the garlic in a garlic press. Drain the olives and chop, or cut into thin slices.
Melt the butter in a frying pan. Cut the cheese into large cubes, place in a food processor and make into a purée on a slow speed, adding first the melted butter, then the cream. Mix the cheese with the other ingredients, season with pepper, heap onto a large dish and arrange the celery sticks around the edge.
The cheese mixture can alternatively be piped into the hollows of the celery sticks using a flat tube, in which case the radishes must be chopped first.

Preparation time: 30 minutes
Finishing time: 10–15 minutes

Veal Salad

1000 grams/35 oz roasted veal
1 bunch flat-leaved parsley
$\frac{1}{2}$ bunch chervil
1 bunch chives
200 grams/7 oz homemade mayonnaise (see p. 44) or fine-quality mayonnaise
3 tablespoons cream
12 black olives
5 anchovy fillets
2 tablespoons capers
2 tablespoons lemon juice
2 tablespoons cognac or brandy
8 tablespoons cold-pressed olive oil
2 tablespoons red wine vinegar
black pepper from the mill
1 lime

Cut the roast veal into 5 mm/$\frac{1}{4}$ inch thick slices, then cut these into 2 cm/1 inch strips.
Wash the herbs and shake dry. Chop the parsley and chervil. Cut the chives across into fine rolls. Mix with the mayonnaise and the cream.
Stone the olives, rinse off the anchovy fillets under cold water, then dab dry.
Place the capers, lemon juice, cognac or brandy, oil and red wine vinegar into the bowl of a food processor, and beat into a smooth sauce (or use a hand-held beater). Season the sauce with pepper. Place the veal strips on to a flat serving dish one next to the other and pour over the light and dark sauces in a trellis fashion. Divide the lemon into segments and garnish the dish with them.

Preparation time: (without making the mayonnaise) 30 minutes
Finishing time: 10 minutes

The Buffet table should contain various breads, such as French sticks, wholegrain breads, pumpernickel, light country bread and three types of crispbreads. Butter balls, preferably served on a bed of crushed ice should be displayed, as well as dripping from roast meat. Drinks, fruit juices, mineral water, beer, and dry light white wine should be served.

Salads as Main Courses

These can be made from interesting ingredients. The gourmet will enjoy, the hearty eater will relish, and the figure-conscious be unable to resist.

Goose Salad with Chestnuts and Apples

400 grams/14 oz roast goose leftovers
200 grams/7 oz canned whole chestnuts
15 grams/$\frac{1}{2}$ oz butter
1 small head of chicory
2 cloves garlic
100 grams/3$\frac{1}{2}$ oz finest quality mayonnaise (or homemade) (see p. 26)
4 tablespoons cream
2 tablespoons yoghurt
salt
3 tablespoons fine salad oil
2 tablespoons lemon juice
1 pinch sugar
white pepper from the mill
2–3 large sharp apples (Jonathan, Boskop, Granny Smith)

Cut the goose flesh (skin removed) into 2 cm/$\frac{3}{4}$ inch cubes.

Drain off the chestnuts and fry off lightly all over in the hot butter.

Clean the chicory, and only use the inside leaves.

Wash the salad and allow to drain off completely in a colander.

Peel the cloves of garlic and pass through a garlic press. Add this to the mayonnaise, and mix in the cream and yoghurt. Season the sauce with salt.

Mix the oil and lemon juice together and season with the sugar, salt and pepper.

Wash the apples, cut into quarters, remove the core and stalk and grate them coarsely. Mix them immediately with the goose flesh, chestnuts and garlic sauce.

Line a large serving dish or salad bowl with the salad leaves and sprinkle with the oil and lemon juice mixture, or toss the salad leaves in it before lining the dish or bowl. Place the goose and chestnut mixture in the centre and serve immediately.

This salad goes well with wholemeal bread and salted butter, but rye bread can be substituted. As a drink, a light dry red wine or a beer would be suitable.

Preparation time: 25 minutes
Finishing time: 15 minutes

<u>Variations:</u> This salad can be made using leftovers of any roasted game, or roast duck. If for example one wished to serve a main dish of duck breast, a whole duck should be bought, and the legs and other parts can be used the following day to prepare the above salad.

Note: Not everyone likes the flavour of garlic. Therefore try the salad made with the following sauce:
125 grams/4 oz mayonnaise flavoured with salt and the grated zest of an untreated orange. This should be seasoned with salt, white pepper and a little ground coriander together with 1 cl/$\frac{1}{3}$ fl oz orange liqueur. This sauce is especially good used with leftover venison or young wild boar used instead of goose.

Chicken Salad with Vegetables

½ package deep-frozen petits pois (150 grams/5 oz)

salt

250 grams/9 oz young carrots

1 grilled chicken (ready-cooked)

2 middle-sized heads fennel

3 sticks celery

2 shallots

1 large bunch dill

150 grams/5 oz finest quality mayonnaise (or homemade) (see p. 26)

3 tablespoons cream

1 egg yolk

1–2 tablespoons strong mustard (Dijon)

1 pinch sugar

a few drops lemon juice

Put the peas into a pan with a little salted water, and cook, covered for about 6 minutes, so that they are not too soft. Drain into a sieve and allow to cool.
Peel the carrots and cut them into fine strips or tiny dice. Blanch them in boiling salted water for 3 minutes. Drain and allow to cool.

Remove the skin from the chicken, if desired, then cut the flesh from the bones and cut into bite-sized pieces.
Clean the fennel and celery, and remove the green leaves, placing them to one side for later use. Wash the fennel and celery and drain off, then cut them both into the same-sized dice as the carrots.
Peel the shallots and chop finely. Rinse the dill, dab it dry and chop it coarsely.
To make the sauce, mix together the mayonnaise, cream, egg yolk and mustard with a whisk. Season with salt, sugar, and lemon juice if desired.
Rinse off the green from the celery and fennel. Dab it dry, then chop. Put half of it, together with the dill into the sauce.

Mix the salad ingredients with the sauce and allow to stand for at least 10 minutes, then add salt to taste, if necessary. Put the salad into a serving dish, and decorate with the rest of the fennel and celery leaves.

This salad tastes good if served with fresh toast, or ovenfresh French bread.

Preparation time: 35 minutes
Finishing time: 15 minutes

Variations: There are many variations of chicken salad, but few predominate. A boiling fowl can be used, but is inferior to a roaster.
It will yield a good stock, which can be used as the basis for other dishes.

Chicken and Cucumber Salad

Cubed or thinly-sliced chicken flesh can be mixed with half a sliced cucumber and 150 grams/5 oz sliced raw mushrooms. Prepare a sauce from soured cream (crème fraîche), a little cream, yoghurt, plenty of puréed garlic and chopped basil. A few cubes of skinned tomatoes should be scattered on top.

Chinese-Style Chicken Salad

50 grams/2 oz of dried morel mushrooms should be soaked in lukewarm water. 1–2 carrots, 200 grams/7 oz canned bamboo shoots and 200 grams/7 oz white cabbage should be cut into very fine strips. Mix all together with 150 grams/5 oz washed and drained soya bean sprouts, the drained morels and the chicken flesh.

Make up a piquant sauce from vinegar (rice vinegar is recommended), soya sauce, groundnut oil, rice wine or dry sherry, and a little sambal oelek, or cayenne pepper.

Chicken Salad with Avocado

Cut flesh from 1 avocado into cubes and mix them immediately with lemon juice. Drain 200 grams/7 oz canned palm hearts and cut them into 1 cm/½ inch thick slices. Mix them both with 200 grams/7 oz canned green asparagus tips and the chicken flesh. Make up a sauce with 1 part each of mayonnaise, soured cream (crème fraîche) and fairly stiffly whipped cream. Season this with salt, white pepper, lemon juice and a little mustard powder. Garnish it with watercress or basil.

111

Apple and White Cabbage Salad

1 small white cabbage (about 500 grams/18 oz)

2 large sharp apples (Jonathan, Granny Smith)

3 shallots

8 tablespoons cold-pressed olive oil (virgin olive oil) or thistle oil

5 tablespoons wine vinegar

salt

black pepper from the mill

$\frac{1}{4}$ teaspoon ground caraway seeds

sugar

$\frac{1}{8}$ litre/4 fl oz dry white wine

1 pink grapefruit

1 untreated lime

$\frac{1}{2}$ red capsicum

1 small green capsicum

2 ripe, but firm bananas

$\frac{1}{4}$ teaspoon strong mustard

Clean the cabbage, then shred it finely, removing the stalk. Peel and quarter the apples, and remove the core and stalk, then cut into 3 mm/$\frac{1}{10}$ inch thick slices.

Peel the shallots, then chop them finely, keeping 1 back, covered.

Put the remaining shallots into a pan with 2 tablespoons oil and fry them off until glazed. Put in the apples of cabbage in alternate layers.

At the same time, sprinkle the cabbage with a little vinegar, and season with salt, pepper and caraway seeds.

Finally sprinkle on a pinch of sugar and pour the wine over the top.

Bring the wine to the boil, and stew the apple–cabbage mixture for 5 minutes in the pan covered with a lid. Then allow to cool.

Peel the grapefruit. Scrub the lime under running water, then remove the zest from the lime with a julienne scraper. Remove the inner white skin, then cut out the flesh in segments with a sharp knife. Remove the thin inner skin from both grapefruit and lime segments.

Clean the capsicums, then wash, dry and cut into thin strips. Peel the bananas and cut into slices.

With the remaining vinegar and oil mix the mustard to make a sauce. Season with salt, pepper and sugar.

Mix the grapefruit and lime segments, capsicums, bananas and the reserved shallot with the sauce.

Line a serving dish with the cooled cabbage—apple mixture, pour over the liquor, then place the grapefruit salad in the centre.

Serve wholegrain bread and butter with this salad. Grilled pork cutlets or roasted chicken legs can also be served with this salad.

Preparation time: (without time for cooling) 35 minutes
Finishing time: 10 minutes

Variation: The basic salad may be prepared using sauerkraut and apples. Canned sauerkraut needs only a short cooking time, and fresh sauerkraut from the barrel needs only to be stewed for 10 minutes. Instead of grapefruit, a mixture of pineapple cubes and skinned blood oranges can be added to the basic salad. Then a piquant sauce can be made from soured cream (crème fraîche), mustard and orange juice and poured over.

Chopped pistachios or walnut kernels should be scattered over the top.

Bremen-style Herring Salad

5 Matjes herring fillets (each about 60 grams/2 oz)

250 grams/9 oz veal

250 grams/9 oz lean pork

salt, white pepper from the mill

40 grams/1½ oz coconut oil

250 grams/9 oz beetroot

250 grams/9 oz potatoes

caraway seeds

1 head celeriac 200 grams/7 oz

3 ready-to-eat Bismarck herrings

3 sharp apples (Boskop, Jonathan, Granny Smith)

3 pickled gherkins

5 hard-boiled eggs

2 tablespoons capers

8 tablespoons wheatgerm oil

5 tablespoons vinegar

sugar

Carefully remove all bones from the Matjes herring fillets using tweezers, then leave them to soak for about 30 minutes in either mineral water, or weak black tea (only if they are very salty).

Rinse the veal and pork, then dry with kitchen tissue, rub with salt and pepper, and separate from one another, brown all over in a frying pan in the hot coconut oil. Moisten with a little hot water, and leave to stew, covered in the pan for about 30 minutes. Allow to cool, then remove from the cooking juices.

While the meat is cooking, prepare the following items. Wash the beetroot and potatoes, then cook separately in water with a little salt and caraway seeds. The beetroot will need about 35 minutes

cooking, the potatoes 25 minutes. Then pour out both, refresh separately under cold water then skin or peel them. Cut the beetroot and potatoes into fine dice. Brush the celeriac and cook in salted water for 35 minutes. Refresh, peel, and cut into dice, as before.

Drain the Matjes fillets and dab dry with kitchen tissue. Halve and skin the Bismarck herring. Cut both of these as well as the peeled cored apples, the hard-boiled eggs and the gherkins into dice. Mix all the above ingredients together with the capers in a large bowl together with their various liquors. Season with the oil, vinegar, salt and pepper together with the meat juices, if desired.

The salad should be left to stand for at least 6 hours, preferably 12 hours, seasoning checked and corrected, and a little more oil added if necessary. Put into a serving dish and serve with freshly-toasted bread.
A light dry white wine or a cool beer would go well with this salad.

Preparation time: (without cooling time) 90 minutes
Finishing time: 15 minutes

Hungarian Sausage Salad

200 grams/7 oz genuine
Hungarian Kolbasz (paprika
sausage)

2 green capsicums

2 red capsicums

2 small onions or 3 shallots

6 firm tomatoes

4 hard-boiled eggs

$\frac{1}{2}$ bunch flat-leaved parsley

1 clove garlic

1 tablespoons herb vinegar

3 tablespoons thick sour cream
or crème fraîche

2 tablespoons cream

2 tablespoons finest quality
mayonnaise

salt, hot paprika

50 grams/1$\frac{3}{4}$ oz coarsely
grated Emmental cheese

1 tablespoon chopped chives

Remove the skin from the
sauce, then cut it in very thin
slices. Wash the capsicums, cut
them at the "seams", remove
the seeds and core, and cut
into fine dice.
Peel the onions or shallots, and
chop or slice thinly into rings.
Blanch the tomatoes, refresh
and skin them, then quarter
and remove seeds, core and
stalk. Cut the quarters lengthwise into halves.
Shell the eggs, and cut into
slices on an egg slicer.
Rinse the parsley, shake dry
and chop it finely.
Pass the peeled garlic through
a garlic press.

Mix the vinegar, soured cream, cream, and mayonnaise into a smooth sauce.
Season with salt and paprika, then mix in the parsley and garlic.
Mix together the capsicums, onions and tomatoes with the sauce.
On a flat serving dish alternate slices of egg with the slices of sausage, and heap the salad in the centre.
Garnish it with the chives and cheese.

Best served with this is a substantial country-style bread with dripping and a cool beer or a strong, red vin de pays.

Preparation time: 20 minutes
Finishing time: 10 minutes

Note: If you cannot obtain the genuine piquant-tasting Kolbasz, replace it with Hungarian salami, scattering over it finely chopped green chili peppers, previously de-seeded, or the small green very hot Hungarian peppers, which can sometimes be purchased in delicatessens.

Hawaii Egg-Salad

200 grams/7 oz fresh or deep-frozen scampi

½ fresh pineapple

200 grams/7 oz canned palm hearts

3 slices (about 5 mm/¼ inch thick) lean cooked ham

6 hard-boiled eggs

3 tablespoons mayonnaise

3 tablespoons soured cream (crème fraîche)

1 tablespoon tomato ketchup

2 tablespoons cream

1 tablespoon cognac

1 tablespoon orange juice

salt, cayenne pepper

½ lettuce

2 firm tomatoes

a few chervil leaves, or

1 teaspoon chopped parsley

Allow the scampi to defrost, then rinse thoroughly in a colander with cold water and drain well.

Peel the pineapple completely removing the "eyes" with a sharp, pointed knife. Cut the fruit lengthwise into eighths, remove the centre core and then cut into small pieces. Drain off the palm hearts and cut into slices about 1 cm/½ inch thick.
Dice the ham. Shell the eggs and slice them using an egg slicer.
Make up a sauce using the mayonnaise, cream, soured cream, tomato ketchup, cognac, and orange juice. Season with salt and cayenne pepper.
Mix the salad ingredients carefully with the sauce, so that the egg slices are not broken. Pull the lettuce to pieces, wash the leaves, and shake dry. Line a serving dish with them and fill the centre with the salad. Blanch the tomatoes with boiling water, refresh with cold, then skin and cut them into 8, removing the seeds, core and stalk.
Wash the chervil, dab dry, and pull the leaves from the stalks. Garnish the salad with the tomato segments and chervil leaves or parsley.

Serve with fresh French bread, or toast with butter, and a light dry white wine, such as a Muller-Thurgau.

Preparation time: (without thawing-out time) 25 minutes
Finishing time: 15 minutes

Note: With egg salads, it is very important that the eggs are completely cooked, otherwise the egg yolk will run, and if too hard, the yolk will crumble. Eggs in weight grade 3 should be cooked for exactly 10 minutes. For each higher weight grade, add 1 minute more cooking time, and for lesser weight grades, deduct 1 minute per grade.

Emmental Egg Salad

Mix the shelled, sliced eggs with 150 grams/5 oz finely cut peg-shaped pieces of Emmental cheese, 150 grams/5 oz diced Bierschinken (ham sausage), 200 grams/7 oz freshly-cooked sliced, peeled jacket potatoes, 2 chopped pickled gherkins (dill pickles), 2 chopped shallots, 1 tablespoon capers, and plenty of chopped fresh herbs.
Add to this a sauce made from sour cream, lemon juice and a little mayonnaise. Garnish with diced tomatoes, or grated young carrots.

What goes with Eggs?

Cooked peas and tuna fish;
Pieces of asparagus, mandarin oranges and finely diced smoked pork loin;
Boiled beef, red and green capsicums and green olives;
Smoked salmon and broccoli florets

Buckling Salad

4 eggs

$\frac{1}{8}$ litre/4 fl oz cream

6 tablespoons milk

salt, white pepper from the mill

grated nutmeg

butter or margarine for greasing

2 bucklings (each about 250 grams/9 oz)

200 grams/7 oz freshly cooked boiled jacket potatoes

$\frac{1}{2}$ cucumber

1 bunch radishes

1 large bunch watercress

2 sharp apples (Boskop, Jonathan, Granny Smith)

5 tablespoons thistle or wheatgerm oil

3 tablespoons very mild vinegar

1 pinch sugar

1 tablespoon small capers

Whisk the eggs with the cream and milk. Season with salt, pepper and nutmeg.
Grease a shallow fireproof dish with butter or margarine. Fill with the egg mixture and cover with aluminium foil. Place in a lightly simmering waterbath and allow to thicken for 20—25 minutes.
In the meantime, skin the buckling, remove the flesh carefully from the backbone and divide into not-too-large pieces. Remove any bones with a pair of tweezers.
Peel the potatoes and halve the washed gherkin removing the seeds. Cut the potatoes and gherkin into fine dice.
Clean the radishes, wash and cut into slices.

Remove the roots from the watercress, wash well in several changes of water, and allow to drain well.

Wash the apples, cut into quarters, peel, remove the core and stalk, then cut into dice. Mix oil and vinegar into a sauce, and season with a little salt, plenty of pepper, and sugar.

Turn out the egg custard, allow it to cool, then cut it into lozenges or rhomboids.

Line a bowl with the watercress. Mix all the salad ingredients except the capers with the sauce and put it into the bowl. Scatter the capers over the top and serve immediately.

Serve with a spicy bread and salted butter, together with a beer.

Preparation time: 35 minutes
Finishing time: (without cooling time) 10 minutes

Variations: Instead of buckling, this salad can be made with smoked fillet of rock salmon or smoked sprats. If a stronger smoked flavour is sought, mackerel fillets can be used. If watercress is not available, use young leaf spinach, or (as in the photo) tender batavia lettuce and $\frac{1}{2}$ carton of mustard and cress can be substituted.

Dietrich Salad

8 artichoke bottoms

8 artichoke hearts

6 small firm tomatoes

4 shallots

4 sticks celery

200 grams/7 oz fresh mushrooms (cèpes (boletus edulis) preferred)

100 grams/3½ oz finest quality mayonnaise

2 tablespoons apple purée

4 tablespoons cream

1–2 tablespoons bottled grated horseradish

a little mild ground paprika

salt, sugar

2 small heads lettuce

2 hard-boiled eggs

2 tablespoons herb vinegar

3 tablespoons finest salad oil

1 tablespoon chopped chives, or ¼ box mustard and cress

Drain the artichoke bottoms and hearts and cut into quarters.
Blanch the tomatoes, skin and quarter them and remove the core and stalk.

Peel the shallots and chop finely, or cut into thin rings. Clean the celery and allow to drain. Cut the stalks into 1 cm/½ inch pieces and chop the leaves, but not too finely. Clean the mushrooms, washing them only if necessary, and drying them completely. Cut them into very fine slices.
Mix together the mayonnaise, apple purée, and cream into a smooth sauce. Season with as much horseradish as desired, paprika, salt and sugar. Mix into the salad.
Remove the outside leaves from the lettuces so that only the light inside leaves remain. Quarter each lettuce. Wash each quarter thoroughly under running water and allow to drain well.
Shell and quarter the eggs. Mix the oil and vinegar together and season with a little salt.
Arrange the lettuce quarters on a serving dish, laying 1 quarter of egg between each eighth of lettuce. Sprinkle the salad leaves and egg with the vinegar and oil sauce, and scatter the top with the chives or mustard and cress.
Heap the salad in the horseradish sauce in the centre.

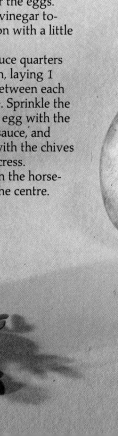

122

This salad goes well with homebaked herb bread, and a light, dry, white wine.

Preparation time: 20 minutes
Finishing time: 15 minutes

Note: If you wish to use this delicate salad as part of a cold buffet, cut all the ingredients into very fine dice, and serve instead of with lettuce and egg, in hollowed-out halves of cucumbers. The salad also lends itself to be used as a starter, in which case the quantities given will be sufficient for 6–8 people. It can also be served in hollowed-out tomatoes, garnished with a slice of egg and half a stuffed olive.

123

Greek Farmer's Salad (Salata Horiatiki)

500 grams/18 oz fully ripe, but firm tomatoes

1 green capsicum

1 red capsicum

1 small cucumber

1 bunch spring onions

75 grams/3 oz each green and black olives

8 anchovy fillets

200 grams/firm white sheep's milk cheese

6 sprigs fresh marjoram

6 sprigs fresh thyme

8 tablespoons cold-pressed olive oil (virgin olive oil)

3 tablespoons herb vinegar

1–2 cloves garlic

salt, black pepper from the mill

Wash tomatoes and capsicums and allow to drain. Cut the tomatoes into eighths, removing the green stalks. Cut the capsicums into quarters and remove the core and seeds, then cut the quarters across into thin strips.
Scrub the cucumber well under running water then cut into slices, but not too thinly.
Clean the spring onions, then cut them into 5 mm/$\frac{1}{4}$ inch rings. Drain off the green and black olives.
Rinse the anchovy fillets under running cold water, then dab them dry. Halve them lengthwise if necessary.
Cut the cheese into 2 cm/1 inch cubes.
Rinse the marjoram and thyme, dry and pull the leaves from the stalks.
Mix all ingredients together in a large bowl.

Mix the oil and vinegar into a smooth sauce.
Peel the garlic and pass through a garlic press. Mix into the sauce and season with a little salt.
Pour the sauce over the salad. Grind plenty of black pepper over the top and serve.

Preparation time: 20 minutes
Finishing time: 10 minutes

Variations: This salad can be prepared using any combination of vegetables depending on the season. In some areas of Greece, slices of courgettes (zucchini) either raw, or stewed for a short time in oil, are used, in other parts, shelled broad beans (favas) or cooked green beans.
Raw sauerkraut (without liquor) can be used, and instead of spring onions, ordinary onions may be substituted.
It is important, however, that olives and sheep's milk cheese are included in the recipe. This salad goes well as an accompaniment to grilled or boiled meats, or grilled fish.

Potato Salad Variations

There are as many recipes for potato salads as there are potatoes in a sack and it is not the intention to repeat all of them here.

Suffice it to say that there are basic recipes, and derivatives from them. In Germany, particularly, there are great differences between north and south. In the north firm salad potatoes are preferred, those that can be mixed with a good mayonnaise sauce, while in the south more mushy types are preferred. In Baden, especially, there is a salad in which the potatoes are so thinly chopped that the finished salad resembles a soup more than a salad, but tastes wonderful. Basically, what are needed for potato salads are previously washed jacket potatoes. It is important that all the tubers are of more or less the same size, so that they cook at the same time. They should be cooked in plenty of salted water, with caraway or dill seeds added, if liked.

The cooked potatoes should be drained, refreshed with cold water, then peeled immediately.

If a "soft" potato salad is required, they should be sliced while hot, then have poured over $\frac{1}{8}$ litre/4 fl oz strongly-flavoured meat stock (from extract or cube) which is to be allowed to soak into them. This quantity will be enough for up to 1000 grams/36 oz potatoes, but more may be added if wished.

If a "firm" potato salad is required, then allow only 10 cl/3$\frac{1}{2}$ fl oz of hot meat stock to floury firmly-cooked potatoes. If using salad potatoes, omit the meat stock, but if desired, the sauce can be made more 'runny''.

Simple Potato Salad

To the basic recipe prepared with the meat stock, add 1–2 finely-chopped onions, and if desired, a clove of garlic passed through a garlic press and the salad allowed to cool. The salad will then be mixed with a sauce made from about 4 tablespoons of wine or herb vinegar, 1 teaspoon mustard, 1 pinch sugar, black pepper and 6–8 tablespoons wheatgerm or corn oil. Herb vinegar is recommended, as the flavour of herbs gives its own distinctive aroma to the salad. The finished salad can be scattered with chopped parsley, chopped chervil or chopped chives.

This simple potato salad will go well with substantial pork roasts, strong types of grilled meats, meat loaves, meat balls, or sausages, grilled or poached, fried fish fillets, or (for children) fish fingers.

Preparation time: (with cooking time) 40 minutes
Finishing time: 10 minutes

Potato and Dandelion Salad

To the simple potato salad leave out the herbs and replace with 75 grams/3 oz young dandelion leaves and 100 grams/3$\frac{1}{2}$ oz crisply fried, diced streaky (belly) bacon. Poached closed blooms could also be added, if liked.

This salad goes well with boiled fish and roast pork with crackling.

Potato and Cucumber Salad

Simple potato salad is prepared with 600 grams/21 oz potatoes and the addition of 1 small unpeeled cucumber, cut into cubes. Omit some of the oil in the dressing and use instead $\frac{1}{8}$ litre/4 fl oz sour cream. Mix the salad with finely-chopped dill.

This salad goes extremely well with fish dishes of all types.

Potato Salad with Mayonnaise

Mix slices of cooked potatoes with a homemade mayonnaise (see p. 27), some sour cream, 2 finely-chopped pickled gherkins (dill pickles) and 2 finely-chopped shallots, and plenty of chopped flat-leaved parsley.

Season with white milled pepper and some salt.

This salad goes well with fried fish fillets, fried sole, with favourite with children, with bockwurst (large smoked frankfurters).

Advice: Commercial mayonnaise sauce (about 150 grams/5 fl oz) can be used in this recipe, but the finished product will have a sharper taste, and will not be so delicate, as with homemade mayonnaise.

Variation: Finely diced, or thinly-sliced celery or celeriac may be added to this salad in quantities according to taste. If celery is used, the leaves may be chopped and mixed into the salad.

The salad can also be made using borage leaves cut into strips and garnished with borage blossoms. Then the salad goes well with poached prime fish.
If the salad is to be used as an accompaniment to roast pork, or boiled brisket of beef, scatter over plenty of freshly-chopped basil, in which case pepper is not necessary.

Pasta Salad Variations

Pasta Salad with Seafood

250 grams/9 oz lumache (snail-shell shaped pasta)
1000 grams/35 oz clams with shells (fresh or deep-frozen)
1000 grams/35 oz mussels
1 bunch soup vegetables
2 onions
1 bunch parsley
$\frac{1}{2}$ litre/18 fl oz dry white wine
250 grams/9 oz squid
2 large leaves of sage
1 sprig rosemary
$\frac{1}{4}$ teaspoon thyme leaves
$\frac{1}{4}$ litre/4 fl oz tomato juice
100 grams/3$\frac{1}{2}$ oz fresh or deep-frozen prawns
1 raw egg yolk
2 hard-boiled egg yolks
3 tablespoons herb vinegar
3 tablespoons olive oil
$\frac{1}{8}$ litre/4 fl oz cream
2 cloves garlic
salt, black pepper from the mill
$\frac{1}{2}$ bunch basil
1 tablespoon small capers

Cook the pasta according to the manufacturer's basic recipe. Scrub the thawed clams and mussels under running water. Discard any that are open. Wash the soup vegetables, then prepare and cut up coarsely.
Peel the onions, cut into eighths, rinse off the parsley. Put all together, with the wine, in a pan and bring to the boil. Put in the mussels and clams, and cook for 10 minutes with the lid on, then drain off. Discard any mussels which are closed, remove the flesh from the remainder.
Rinse off the thawed-out squid, and cut the flesh into bite-sized pieces.
Rinse off the sage, rosemary and thyme, put them together with the squid and the tomato juice into a closed pan and stew for 15 minutes. Pour off the juice.
Rinse off the prawns in cold water and allow to drain off completely. (Deep-frozen ones must be completely thawed first.)
Mix the raw egg yolk with the cooked, which has been passed through a sieve, the vinegar, oil and cream to make a creamy sauce.
Pass the peeled garlic cloves through a garlic press and add to the sauce, then season with salt and pepper.
Mix all the ingredients together.
Rinse the basil, dab it dry, and pull the leaves from the stalk.
Scatter the basil and the capers over the salad.

Preparation time: (without time for thawing) 45 minutes
Finishing time: 15 minutes

American Style Pasta Salad

Mix the cooked pasta with 200 grams/7 oz canned sweet

corn, 200 grams/7 oz cooked bacon rashers cut into strips, 1 bunch of radishes sliced, ½ diced cucumber, and 4 chopped hard-boiled eggs. Add a sauce made from mayonnaise flavoured with chili sauce and finely diced red and green capsicums, or Thousand Island dressing (see p. 29).

Preparation time: 15 minutes
Finishing time: 10 minutes

Pasta and Tuna Fish Salad

Mix the prepared pasta with the drained, broken-up flesh from a large can of tuna, having saved the oil from the can.
Add to this oil 1 bunch chopped flat-leaved parsley, 2–3 finely-sliced sticks of celery, together with 1 chopped celery leaf, 1 finely-diced root of fennel together with its finely-chopped leaves, 1 grated carrot, 2 skinned, de-seeded, finely-chopped tomatoes and 2 tablespoons capers.
Add as much vinegar as desired in order to make a smooth sauce, seasoning it with 1 garlic clove pressed through a garlic press, salt and black milled pepper. Mix the sauce into the salad.
This salad looks especially good when made with green tagliatelle.

Preparation time: 20 minutes
Finishing time: 10 minutes

Rice-Salad Variations

Basic Preparation

200 grams/7 oz long-grain rice

a good $\frac{1}{2}$ litre/18 fl oz meat stock

Put the rice and stock into an open pan and bring to the boil. Put on the lid, and cook for 20 minutes on a very low heat, then allow to cool. During the cooking period, stir frequently, in order that the grains do not stock together.

For rice salad, it is recommended to use converted rice which is available commercially. This is parr-boiled to remove some of the surface starch, but retains its full complement of vitamins and nutrients, and does not stick together.

Indian-Style Rice Salad

Rice according to the basic recipe

200 grams/7 oz fresh or deep-frozen shrimps

5 slices canned pineapple

250 grams/9 oz fresh apricots

4 bottled ginger plums

50 grams/$1\frac{3}{4}$ oz flaked almonds

10 grams/$\frac{1}{3}$ oz butter

2 bananas

2 tablespoons lemon juice

2 tablespoons mango chutney

150 grams/5 oz finest quality mayonnaise

4 tablespoons cream

salt

strong curry paste

a few mint or chervil leaves

Allow the rice to cool. Rinse the shrimps briefly in cold water and drain in a colander. (Allow deep-frozen ones to thaw first.)
Cut the pineapple slices into small pieces.
Blanch the apricots in boiling water, remove the skins and stones and cut into eighths.
Cut the ginger plums into slices.
Fry the almond flakes in hot butter in a frying pan until golden brown, stirring all the time, and allow to cool.
Peel the bananas, cut into slices, then place them immediately into the lemon juice, so that they do not discolour.
Chop the chutney if necessary.
Mix the mayonnaise with the cream into a smooth sauce. Season with salt and as much curry as desired.
Mix all ingredients except the almond flakes into the sauce. Scatter the almond flakes and the mint- or chervil leaves over the top of the salad.
In half-quantities, this salad would go well as a starter.

Preparation time: (without time to cook the rice)
25 minutes
Finishing time: 10 minutes

Balkan-Style Rice Salad

Mix the cooked rice with 100 grams/$3\frac{1}{2}$ oz finely-chopped raw sauerkraut, 1 preserved red capsicum, 1 preserved green capsicum, 4 skinned, de-seeded tomatoes cut into strips, 2 tablespoons chopped chives, 2 finely-chopped cloves of garlic, 100 grams/$3\frac{1}{2}$ oz quartered canned small mushrooms and 75 grams/$2\frac{1}{2}$ oz grated Emmental cheese.
Mix 200 grams/7 oz thick, sour cream with salt and ground sweet paprika, and pour it over the salad.

Preparation time: 30 minutes
Finishing time: 5 minutes

Green Rice Salad

Mix the cooked rice with half an unpeeled cucumber cut into fine dice. Add to this, 1 bunch chopped seasonal herbs, 4 spring onions cut into little rolls, 150 grams/5 oz crunchy, cooked princess beans, 150 grams/5 oz cooked deep-frozen green peas, and 200 grams/7 oz diced cooked ham.
Pass 2 hard-boiled eggs through a sieve, add 1 teaspoon strong mustard, 4 tablespoons vinegar, and 8 tablespoons oil and some salt, to make a smooth sauce. Pour the sauce over the salad. Garnish with radish rosettes.

Preparation time: 35 minutes
Finishing time: 10 minutes

The Sweetest Fruits for the Best Desserts

Fruit is a pleasure to everyone,
whether exotic from foreign lands,
or home grown, on its own, or
combined with other varieties to make
mouth-watering dishes.

Exotic Winter Salad

200 grams/7 oz fresh dates

1 small fresh pineapple

2 sharon-kakis (persimmons)

200 grams/7 oz Cape gooseberries

1 pomegranate

1 carton sour cream

2 teaspoons icing sugar (confectioner's) sugar

2 cl/¾ fl oz orange liqueur

1 large pinch cinnamon

Skin the dates, then halve and remove the stones.

Remove the stalk and crown from the pineapple, then peel the fruit thickly, removing the "eyes" with the point of a sharp knife. Cut the fruit lengthwise into eighths, then cut out the hard centre, after which cut the fruit into fine dice.

Wash the kaki fruit thoroughly and dry. Remove the leaf and stalk with the point of a sharp knife. The fruit can be cut, as desired either into slices or eighths. Remove the Cape gooseberries from their outside skins, rinse and dry well.

Halve the pomegranate and remove the seeds with a tea-spoon. This is best done over a bowl, in order to catch the juice. Put the seeds to one side. Beat the cream until fairly firm, then add the icing sugar, little by little, the pomegranate juice, liqueur and cinnamon. Mix all ingredients together with half the cream and put into a glass bowl, or individual dishes. Pour over the re-maining cream and sprinkle with the pomegranate seeds. Serve immediately.

Preparation time: 15 minutes
Finishing time: 10 minutes

Note: If you find that the pomegranate seeds are too hard, and you still wish to add the flavour of this fruit, just use the juice. Place the seeds into a hair sieve, and press them well to release the juice. If the fruit is too hard, roll the fruit on a hard surface until the flesh becomes soft to the touch, then make a hole in the side and squeeze the fruit to allow the juice to flow out.

<u>Variation:</u> If you are unable to obtain fresh dates (they are exported from Israel between October and May deep-frozen and thawed out before sale) dried dates may be used, in which case use half-quantity and chop coarsely.

<u>Advice:</u> Cape gooseberries bear no resemblance to domestic gooseberries, except the name, as they are a far-removed relation to the tomato (solanum). They are usually imported from Kenya or Madagascar from December to June.

Pawpaw Salad

2 ripe pawpaws

200 grams/7 oz sugar

scraped-out pith from $\frac{1}{2}$ vanilla pod

$\frac{1}{8}$ litre/4 fl oz water

2 tablespoons bottled ginger syrup

1 small pinch ground cloves

1 pinch cinnamon

1 grapefruit

4 preserved ginger plums

juice of 1 lemon

2 cl/$\frac{3}{4}$ fl oz white rum

2 tablespoons pine kernels

Peel and halve the pawpaws, remove the black seeds with a spoon. Cut the fruit into thin strips. Place in a pan together with the water, sugar, vanilla pith, ginger syrup, ground cloves, and cinnamon. Bring to the boil, then allow to simmer gently for 10–15 minutes until the strips are soft, and the liquor has almost boiled away. Allow to cool.
Peel the grapefruit and remove the inner skin. Cut out the fruit segments with a sharp knife, removing the membrane between each segment.
Chop the ginger plums coarsely.
Mix the rum and lemon juice together.
Arrange the grapefruit segments in a star-shape on a flat dish.

Mix the pawpaw strips and their syrup together with the rum and lemon mixture, and place in the centre of the grapefruit segments.
Scatter the pine kernels on top.

Preparation time: (without cooking time) 10 minutes
Finishing time: (without cooling time) 10 minutes

Note: If this salad is flavoured instead with a little powdered ginger, it will go well as an accompaniment to curry or game dishes. If tamarillos (tree tomatoes) can be obtained, these can be used in this salad. With their light, bitter but sour flavour they contrast well with the sweet flavour of the pawpaws.

Pawpaws, which belong to the large melon family, originate in Mexico, but are today cultivated in nearly all tropical and sub-tropical lands.

Imported fruit have an average weight of 500 grams/18 oz each but some can weigh as much as 9 kilos/20 lbs! Pawpaws are very sensitive, and spoil quickly. That is why only the most robust types are exported, and are shipped underripe, so that they ripen on the journey, and are often underripe when sold. If fruit needs to be ripened, do not place it in the refrigerator. It is best left at room temperature in a place with high humidity. When ripe, the fruit has yellow spots on the skin and gives under finger pressure. Then the fruit has a deep orange tone and is soft as butter.

Mixed Fruit Salad

2 oranges

2 seedless mandarins or
clementines

1 winter pear

2 small sweet/sour apples
(Cox's orange or Jonathan)

1 large or 2 small bananas

50 grams/1¾ oz fine sugar

1 packet vanilla sugar

juice of ½ lemon

50 grams/1¾ oz chopped
walnut kernels

Peel the oranges, removing all
the inner skin. Remove the
segments, using a sharp knife,
and cutting away all the membrane between the segments.
Keep a few for garnishing, and
dice the rest.
Peel the mandarins or clementines in a similar manner and
remove the threads of skin.
Leave the segments whole, or
halve them, as desired.
Peel the washed apples and
pear, remove core and quarter
them, then remove pips, and
cut into fine dice.
Peel the bananas, quarter
lengthwise, and dice the flesh.

Mix all the ingredients together with the sugar, vanilla
sugar, lemon juice. Allow to
stand for 10 minutes.
Dress the fruit salad into a
bowl and garnish with the
orange segments. Scatter the
walnut segments over the top.

Preparation time: 20 minutes
Finishing time: (without
standing time) 5 minutes

Advice: This salad is rich in
vitamins and is therefore
extremely healthy, especially
in winter. Being rich in vitamin
C is helps fight off colds and
influenza.
If more vitamins are desired,
add 1−2 sliced kiwi fruit to the
salad. One kiwi fruit will
supply the daily needs of
vitamin C for 1 person. If
concern for a few extra calories
is not important, freshly-
whipped cream or creamy
beaten soured cream (crème
fraîche) can improve the salad.
A shot of Advokaat, raspberry
liqueur or kirsch will improve
the flavour of the salad if
desired.

Persimmon Salad with Mango Sauce

1 large ripe mango
50 grams/1¾ oz sugar
1 pinch ground ginger
1 pinch ground cloves
6 kiwi fruit
6 kumquats
2 persimmons (kakis)
1 tablespoon crushed cracknel (commercial product)

Cut the skin of the mango several times lengthwise, so that it can be pulled off in strips.
Loosen the flesh around the stone so that it can can be removed. Cut the flesh into large cubes. Mix it with the sugar, ginger, and cloves and put into a pan long enough for the sugar to dissolve, mixing all the time.
Put the mixture into the bowl of a food processor, or use a hand mixer to produce a purée. Keep the sauce lukewarm.
Peel the kiwis and slice thinly. Scrub the kumquats, dry them off and cut them into slices, removing any pips.
Wash the kakis, dry them and with a sharp knife remove the stalk out of the fruit. Cut them also into thin slices.
Arrange the kaki slices in a petal-shape around 4 dessert plates, then arrange the kiwi slices, and finally the kumquat slices on top. Pour over the mango sauce, and decorate with the crushed cracknel.

Serve immediately.

Preparation time: 25 minutes
Finishing time: 5 minutes

Kakis (persimmons) originate in Asia, but today are cultivated in both Israel and Italy. Italian kakis taste best when they are soft as butter, when they must be eaten with a spoon. The Israeli type when ripe has a firm flesh which will permit slicing. Italian kakis are sold from October until November, while Israeli kakis are sold from November to January.

Kumquats are dwarf oranges that have only been available fresh for a few years. Previously they were only sold in syrup. Really fresh kumquats are delightful in flavour. The whole fruit can be eaten, but the pips must be removed. They are not eaten peeled, as the skin has the most intensive flavour, and is often sweeter than the inside.

Grape and Nut Salad in Pineapple Boats

250 grams/9 oz black dessert grapes

250 grams/9 oz white dessert grapes

2 cl/$\frac{3}{4}$ fl oz each of cognac or brandy, kirsch, cointreau, and maraschino

1 small fresh pineapple of about 1000 grams/35 oz (weighed with leaf-crown)

1 orange

1 lemon

50 grams/1$\frac{3}{4}$ oz icing (confectioner's) sugar

a few drops vanilla extract

100 grams/3$\frac{1}{2}$ oz hazelnut kernels

$\frac{1}{8}$ litre/4 fl oz cream

1 tablespoon chocolate strands (vermicelli) (commercial product)

Wash the grapes. Allow to drain well, then pull the berries from the stalks. Halve the grapes and remove the pips. Mix the liqueurs together and place in the grapes. Cover and allow to steep for about 30 minutes in the refrigerator. Remove the stalk from the pineapple without cutting into the fruit. Cut the fruit in halves lengthwise leaving the leaf crown on each half.
Cut out the fruit from each half with a sharp knife. Remove the hard centre part and dice the remainder.
Add to the grapes and allow to stand for a further 15 minutes.
Squeeze the orange and lemon and add the juice to the icing sugar, seasoning with the vanilla extract.
Sprinkle half on to the pineapple shells and place these in the refrigerator.
Roast the hazelnut kernels in a non-stick pan without fat until they are golden brown and their skins become brittle and come off easily. Rub the nuts in a kitchen cloth and allow to cool.

In between times, whip the cream very stiff.
Mix the grapes and pineapple with the nuts, half of the cream and the remaining orange-lemon juice mixture and fill into the pineapple halves.
Put the rest of the cream into a piping bag fitted with a star tube and decorate the salad with it. Finally garnish the salad with the chocolate strands, and serve immediately.

Preparation time: (without standing time) 20 minutes
Finishing time: 15 minutes

Variation: Instead of serving in hollowed-out pineapple halves with diced pineapple, this salad

can be presented in hollowed-out melon halves and served with melon balls. This should be done using 2 middle-sized Ogen melons prepared as described on page 150. They should be cut with zig-zagged tops (Vandyked) and the melon flesh allowed to steep with the grapes in the liqueur. Each portion will be served in 1 melon half.

143

Strawberry Salad with Pepper-Cream

500 grams/18 oz small
aromatic strawberries

100 grams/$3\frac{1}{2}$ oz sugar

4 cl/$1\frac{1}{2}$ fl oz raspberry liqueur

1 carton cream
(200 grams/7 oz)

2 teaspoons preserved green
peppercorns

Wash the strawberries, allow
to drain spread on a thick layer
of kitchen tissue. Carefully dry
them with tissue, then remove
the stalks. Cut the fruit in
halves lengthwise.
Mix with the sugar and leave
for a good 60 minutes at room
temperature to allow the juices
to flow. Mix them from time
to time so that the sugar will
all dissolve.
Mix the strawberries then with
the liqueur and cover the bowl
with cling film and leave it in
the refrigerator for 30 minutes.
Meanwhile beat the cream
stiff. Allow the peppercorns to
drain and chop them roughly.
Mix them into the cream. Fill
the cream into a piping tube
fitted with a large star tube.
Divide the berries into 4
portion dishes and pipe a large
cream rosette in the middle of
each.

This salad goes well with a dry
sparkling wine or a medium
dry sherry.

Preparation time: (without
standing time) 15 minutes
Finishing time: 15 minutes

Note: This salad is especially
good if the most aromatic
strawberries are used, but even
better are wild strawberries, if
obtainable. Unfortunately,
these are rarely obtainable in
the market, and if so, at
enormous prices.

At the end of May, when the
first ripe strawberries appear,
fresh woodruff may be
available. Try replacing the
peppercorns with this aromatic
herb.

Orange and Strawberry Salad

5 small juicy oranges

2 cl/$\frac{3}{4}$ fl oz cognac or brandy

4 cl/$1\frac{1}{2}$ fl oz cointreau

200 grams/7 oz small
strawberries

$\frac{1}{8}$ litre/4 fl oz cream

2 tablespoons Amaretto di
Saronno liqueur (Italian
almond liqueur)

Peel the oranges like an apple
so as to remove the white
inner skin.
Then cut across into slices, removing any pips. Arrange the
slices on a dish overlapping,
like roof tiles. Mix the cognac
or brandy with the cointreau
and sprinkle all over the
orange slices. Cover the
orange slices with clingfilm
and keep in a cool place, but
not in the refrigerator. Allow
to stand for 30 minutes.
Wash the strawberries, dry
well, then remove the stalks.
Beat the cream stiff, then add
the Amaretto little by little. Fill
the cream into a piping bag
fitted with a small star tube.
Arrange the strawberries on
the orange slices and decorate
with cream rosettes or a cream
border.
Serve this salad with delicate
almond biscuits.

Preparation time: (without
time for standing) 20 minutes
Finishing time: 10 minutes

Cranberry and Orange Salad

250 grams/9 oz fresh
cranberries (see below)

125 grams/4½ oz sugar

1 pinch ground coriander

20 grams/¾ oz flaked almonds

4 small oranges

4 cl/1½ fl oz orange liqueur

¼ litre/9 fl oz cream

1 packet vanilla sugar

Wash and drain off the cranberries. Mix them with the sugar and coriander in a pan large enough that they can simmer until the sugar has dissolved and the first berries begin to burst.
Remove the pan from the stove and place it into a cold water bath containing some ice cubes and allow to cool. Roast the almonds until golden brown in a non-stick pan, shaking them frequently, then allow them to cool. Peel the oranges like apples, removing the inner skin, then cut the fruit across into slices. Remove any pips. Mix with the liqueur and leave for 20 minutes for the flavours to mingle.

Beat the cream until stiff adding the vanilla extract little by little.
Mix the cream with half the cranberries. Arrange the orange slices onto a serving dish and put the cranberry/cream mixture into the centre. Arrange the rest of the cranberries around the outside. Scatter the cream with the almonds.

Preparation time: (without time for cooling) 10 minutes
Finishing time: (without standing time) 10 minutes

Variation: Cranberries are related distantly to the moss berries of the Continent. Cranberries are usually imported from the U.S.A., but they are also cultivated in Holland and Poland.
They were first cultivated in large quantities about 50 years ago and have a slightly bitter sour flavour, but otherwise are milder than the continental product. Through their large pectin content they gel very easily. They can be stored cooked for weeks in a refrigerator.

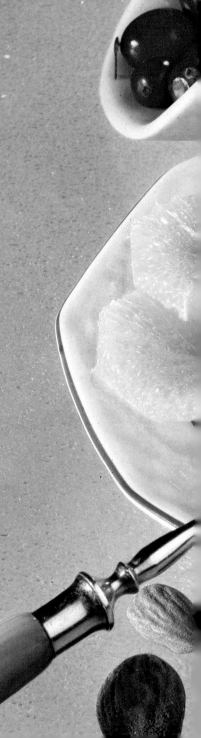

Rum-Pot Fruit Salad with Meringue Topping

2 oranges

1 sour apple

2 canned peach halves

2 slices canned pineapple

4 tablespoons rum-pot fruits

4 tablespoons rum-pot liquor

3 egg whites

½ teaspoon lemon juice

125 grams/4 oz sugar

1 packet vanilla sugar

50 grams/1¾ oz ground almonds

Peel the oranges and apple. Remove the white skin from the oranges, then cut the fruit across into thin slices, and remove pips if necessary. Remove the stalk and blossom end from the apple and cut out the core.

Slice the apple also. Cut the drained peach halves into thin wedges and the pineapple slices into dice.

Put all the fruit onto a flat ovenproof dish and place the rum-pot fruit into the centre. Sprinkle the fruit with the rum-pot liquor.

Mix the egg white and lemon juice and beat until stiff, adding little by little the sugar and the vanilla sugar beating until the sugar has all dissolved.

Fill the meringue mixture into a piping bag fitted with a star tube.

Pipe the meringue in a spiral, starting from the centre of the dish to cover the whole of the fruit, then place the dish in a pre-heated oven at 180°C/350°F (gas mark 4) for 45–50 minutes, until the peaks of the meringue are beginning to become brown.

Allow the meringue to cool somewhat, then serve at once. This dish will go well with Mocha, Espresso or a dry sparkling wine.

Preparation time: 25 minutes
Finishing time: (without baking time) 10 minutes

Note: As rum-pot fruits are not always available, a quick method of preparing "rum cherries" can be used.

Take some canned stoneless morello cherries. Allow them to drain, keeping the liquor from the can. Pour over some Jamaica Rum, cover with clingfilm and allow to stand overnight. On the following day, allow to drain off again and use as rum-pot fruit.

The rum, together with as much of the liquor as desired, can be mixed and poured over the fruit.

Note: A rum-pot is a favourite method used in Germany of preserving fruit in rum to be consumed in winter.

Melon Salad

1 watermelon, or 1 honeydew melon

1 canteloupe melon

1 ogen melon

$\frac{1}{8}$ litre/4 fl oz medium dry sherry (amontillado or oloroso)

2 untreated blood oranges

2 tablespoons icing sugar (confectioner's) sugar

2 tablespoons cognac or brandy

$\frac{1}{8}$ litre/4 fl oz cream

1 packet vanilla sugar

20 grams/$\frac{3}{4}$ oz flaked almonds

Halve all 3 melons. From the canteloupe and ogen melons remove the soft central flesh and seeds with a spoon. Remove the first outside flesh with a pommes Parisienne cutter (ball cutter). Cut out the flesh from the watermelon in the same way, removing the black seeds as you go.
Put all the melon balls into a large bowl and mix with the sherry, then fill it into 2–3 melon halves. Cover with clingfilm and leave to stand for at least 3 hours, but preferably 6 hours, in the refrigerator to cool through.
Scrub the oranges under running water, dry them, then remove the skin in thin strips, using a zester. Squeeze the juice from the oranges. Remove the melon balls from the bowl, saving the juice. Mix 3 tablespoons of the juice with the orange juice and the cognac or brandy.
Fill the melon balls again into the melon halves and pour over the juice mixture. Cover

again with clingfilm and return to the refrigerator for a further 30 minutes to mingle the flavours.
Beat the cream until stiff, adding the vanilla sugar, little by little. Put the cream into a piping bag fitted with a star tube. Garnish the filled melon halves with rosettes of cream and scatter these with strands of orange peel. Finish off by scattering the tops of the melons with the flaked almonds. Serve immediately. This salad will go well with delicate pastries and moka coffee, or a favourite sparkling wine.

Preparation time: (without time for cooling) 20 minutes
Finishing time: (without time for standing) 15 minutes

Note: Add the remaining sherry/melon juice mixture to a sparkling wine to make a good long drink.

Variation: Instead of the canteloupe or ogen melon, quartered figs or small canned figs can be added to the salad. The salad also tastes good if lychees or fresh strawberries are added.
A special touch is given to the salad if garden blackberries are used, and the cognac or brandy is substituted by raspberry liqueur (himbeergeist), as flavouring.

Melons are "children of the sun", and thanks to modern transport methods it is possible to obtain them almost all year round.

There are 2 basic types of melon, the watermelon and the sweet melons.
Watermelons consist of up to 95% water and have flesh which can vary from pink to dark red, with hard, black seeds embedded in it. The fruit is very refreshing but does not have a very intense flavour.
Sweet melons on the contrary have, when ripe, a very intense aroma which will vary from type to type. These melons can be divided into 3 main sorts: the smooth melons, the "netted" melons and the canteloupes. All have similar characteristics: the seeds are situated as in a marrow, surrounded by a thread-like or soft, inedible flesh, in the middle of the fruit. The smooth melons are best-known by the ubiquitous, rugby-football shaped *honeydew* melon. The canteloupe melons derive their

name from a village in the vicinity of Rome and they are smooth-skinned, but ribbed. They are the best-known of this type, and should be eaten at the latest 1 week after harvesting. The finest of all of this family is the French charentais melon.

Netted melons have, as their name implies, a skin which appears to be covered with a white to brown net according to the variety. One of the most aromatic of this type is the Israeli-cultivated Ogen melon, which is available from April to December.

Pear Salad with Curd Cheese Dressing

4 large juicy pears

3 tablespoons lemon juice

2 tablespoons pear liqueur (Poire Williams)

100 grams/3½ oz double cream curd cheese

4 tablespoons cream

2 tablespoons bottled raw cranberries

coarsely-ground pepper

1 small pinch ground coriander

150 grams/5 oz black dessert grapes

25 grams/¾ oz walnut kernels

Peel and quarter the pears. Remove the stalk and core. Cut the quarters into 4 thick even slices.
Mix the lemon juice and the liqueur together and turn the pear slices in it. Arrange the slices in star fashion on a serving dish or 4 portion dishes. Sprinkle the rest of the liquid over the top of the pear slices. Cover with clingfilm and leave in the refrigerator to soak for 30 minutes.

Break up the curd cheese with a fork and mix with the cream and cranberries to produce a smooth mass. Season with the pepper and coriander.
Wash the grapes and dry well. Pull the fruit from the stalks, halve and remove the pips. Mix carefully into the cheese dressing and place in the middle of the pear slices. Garnish with the walnut kernels. Mix together only when ready to eat.
Puff pastry cheese cakes go well with this salad and also a medium-dry or cream sherry.

Preparation time: (without time for soaking) 25 minutes
Finishing time: 5 minutes

Apple Salad with Cranberry Sauce

4 sour apples

$\frac{1}{8}$ litre/4 fl oz white wine

50 grams/$\frac{3}{4}$ oz sugar

$\frac{1}{4}$ stick cinnamon

2 cloves

1 untreated orange

4 tablespoons bottled cranberry sauce

2 tablespoons medium dry sherry (amontillado)

1 tablespoon cognac or brandy

1 small pinch powdered ginger

1 tablespoon shelled pistachio nuts

Peel the apples. Remove the cores with an apple corer. Cut the apples across into slices about 5 mm/$\frac{1}{4}$ inch thick.
Bring the wine, sugar, cloves and cinnamon to the boil. Lay in the apple slices and simmer for a bare 5 minutes. Remove with a skimmer and allow to cool.
Scrub the orange under running water, then dry and grate the zest.
Squeeze the juice from the orange. Mix the juice with the cranberries, sherry and cognac or brandy. Flavour with the ginger.
Arrange the apple slices on 4 individual dishes. Pour over the cranberry sauce. Scatter the orange rind and pistachios on top.

Preparation time: (without cooling time) 20 minutes
Finishing time: 5 minutes

Note: For this salad use sweet—sour apples only, such as Boskop, Jonathan, Cox's Orange, or Red Delicious, rather than very sweet apples, as they lose their flavour in the cooking. In buying apples sometimes the less attractive fruit make the best buy, especially if they are used for cooking.

Nectarine and Kiwi-Fruit Salad

4 nectarines
4 kiwi fruit
200 grams/7 oz black grapes
200 grams/7 oz strawberries
4 cl/1½ fl oz maraschino liqueur
2 tablespoons icing sugar (confectioner's) sugar
25 grams/¾ oz chopped hazelnuts
1 small carton soured cream (crème fraîche) (100 grams/3½ oz)

Dip the nectarines momentarily into boiling water, then refresh with cold water and skin the fruit (see below). Halve the fruit, remove the stones then cut into thin wedges. Peel the kiwi fruit and cut into 3 mm/⅛ inch slices. Wash the grapes, leave to drain, halve and remove the pips.

Carefully wash the strawberries, lay them on a thick layer of kitchen tissue, dab them dry, then remove the stalks, and according to size, cut into halves or quarters. Mix the liqueur with the icing sugar until the sugar has dissolved. Mix the prepared fruit with the liqueur and leave it covered in the refrigerator for 30 minutes to soak. Fry the hazelnuts in a non-stick pan without fat until golden brown. Beat the soured cream with an electric or hand whisk until creamy. Turn the fruit, then fill into a serving dish and heap the soured cream in the centre. Scatter the hazelnuts over the top. Mix only when ready to eat.

Preparation time: 15 minutes
Finishing time: (without time for soaking) 10 minutes

Variation: Peaches can be substituted for the nectarines. The best to be recommended are the white-fleshed Italian or domestic peaches, but they must really be skinned, whereas the nectarines only need skinning if the skin is thick.
Nectarines are akin to peaches, being a cross between peaches with their velvety skin, and plums. They have, in general a firmer flesh than "true" peaches.
Kiwi fruit originated in China, and were often called Chinese gooseberries. Today they are mainly imported from New Zealand where they have been grown for the last 70 years in large plantations. The New Zealanders gave them the name "kiwi" after a strange, flightless bird that the Maoris, the original inhabitants, named kiwi.

Stewed Fig Salad

8 fresh dark figs

4 cl/1½ fl oz crème de cassis (blackcurrant liqueur)

6 cl/2 fl oz white wine

150 grams/5¼ oz deep-frozen raspberries

1 tablespoon icing sugar (confectioner's) sugar

2 ripe peaches

Wash, dry and quarter the figs. Mix the blackcurrant liqueur and the wine in a pan and lay in the figs, cut side down, and stew for 10 minutes with the lid on.
Pass the thawed-out raspberries through a hair sieve, so that the pips are retained in the sieve. Mix the raspberry pulp with the icing sugar.
Put the peaches into boiling water for a couple of moments, then take out, refresh and skin them. Cut in halves, remove the stones and cut into chunks.
Take out the fig halves and arrange the 8 segments in a star shape on a dessert plate. Allow the fig-liquor to cool. Put the peach chunks into a food processor or use the cutter blade on a hand-held mixer and make into a fine purée, adding the fig-liquor little by little.
Pour the raspberry purée on one half of the dish and the peach purée on the other half. Serve with almond biscuits and a glass of demi-sec sparkling wine.

Variation: Instead of fresh figs, canned figs can be used. In this case allow 5—6 figs per person as they are usually very small.

Leave the uncut figs to soak in the blackcurrant/wine mixture overnight, then proceed as above, including the peach purée.
The blackcurrant/wine mixture can be substituted by 6 cl/2 fl oz Amaretto liqueur (Italian almond liqueur) or 8 cl/3 fl oz vodka.

Preparation time: 30 minutes
Finishing time: 5 minutes

Pineapple Salad with Lime Cream

1 fresh pineapple (about 1200 grams/42 oz)

2 untreated limes

1 carton sour cream (200 grams/7 oz)

2 tablespoons icing sugar (confectioner's) sugar

pith from ¼ vanilla pod, or few drops vanilla extract

Remove the leaf-crown from the pineapple and the stalk. With the pine standing up-right, remove the skin thickly with a sharp knife, removing the "eyes" with the point of the knife.
Cut the pineapple into eighths lengthwise, remove the hard centre core and cut the flesh into 3 cm/1½ inch thick pieces. Scrub the limes under running water, dry, then cut 1 lime into thin slices. From the second lime, cut the skin into thin strips using a zester or a very sharp knife, then squeeze the juice from the fruit.

Beat the cream half-stiff, adding the icing sugar and vanilla or extract while beating. When nearly beaten add as much lime juice as liked to flavour and mix in half of the zest.
Arrange the slices of lime on the edge of a plate, petal-fashion, heaping the pineapple chunks in the centre. Pour over the cream. Scatter the rest of the zest over the top.
Serve with Mocha or Espresso coffee.

Variation: Instead of pineapple, this dessert can be made with mango cubes. In this case do not serve alcohol, as it does not go with this fruit. If no limes are available, use instead slices of untreated oranges.
This dessert can be scattered with lightly roasted grated coconut instead of fruit zest.

Preparation time: 25 minutes
Finishing time: 10 minutes

Salads and their Culinary Uses

	FISH AND SHELLFISH 	PORK 	LAMB AND MUTTON 
Lettuce	With sauce made from cream or soured cream	With escalopes and cutlets	With stews and rolled roasts
Oak Leaf Salad or Batavia Lettuce	With vinaigrette made from sherry vinegar	With a delicate oil/vinegar sauce for fillet	With a delicate vinaigrett for saddles
Lamb's Lettuce	With yoghurt or cream/herb sauce	With a sweet/sour sauce for fillets	With vinaigrette for cutlets and leg
Curly Endive or Scarole	With a strong herb vinaigrette	With a herb/yoghurt sauce for all roasts	As green salad
Radicchio		Mixed with iceberg lettuce for fillets	With vinaigrette for cutlets and saddles
Chicory	With vinaigrette for fish fillets	With fillets, escalopes and stuffed rolled roasts	
Cos Lettuce	With a strong herb sauce	With cutlets and roast loin	As radicchio
Spinach (as salad)	With poached prime fish and scampi	With all types of grills	
Chinese Leaf	With pineapple chunks and orange pieces for stronger flavoured fish	With apples and bananas for meat loaf	With grapes in yoghurt dressing for saddle of lamb
White Cabbage or Red Cabbage (as salad)		With pig's feet, ribs and roasts	
Tomatoes	Only with grilled fish	Mixed with cucumber and capsicums for grills	With all substantial mutton dishes
Cucumbers	With fried fish		As tomatoes, mixed with strong cheese sauce
Celery	With shellfish and prime fish	For fillets and escalopes	In mixed salads with roasts
Celeriac		Cooked, in vinaigrette for all roasts	
Green Beans (cooked)		For loin roasts and ham roasts	With all lamb and mutton dishes
Radishes		With substantial roasts, pig's feet and meat balls	With rolled roasts
Carrots			Mixed with cauliflower for leg joints
Cauliflower		Cooked, with pig's feet	
Potatoes (boiled)	With egged and bread-crumbed fried fish	With smoked loin, pig's feet and ribs	With all grilled meat dishes
Capsicums	Skinned, in vinaigrette with fried fish		With all dishes of Mediterranean origin

EEF	VEAL	POULTRY	GAME	EGG DISHES
...ith all boiled cuts	With any sauce for all dishes	With roast and grilled chicken	Only with stews	With all egg dishes
...ith fillet, rump steak and ...oasts	With fillet, escalopes and steaks	With delicate feathered game	With all fillets and roasts	With poached eggs and herb omelettes
...s oak leaf salad	As oak leaf salad	As oak leaf salad and with poultry breasts of all sorts	As oak leaf salad	As lettuce and oak leaf lettuce
...s lettuce	With rolled stuffed breast of veal	With strongly-flavoured roasted joints	Endive with stews, Scarole as oak leaf lettuce	As lettuce
...ith vinaigrette for ...autéed meats	Mixed with chicory for escalopes, steaks and roasts	With oak leaf salad for pigeon, pheasants, guinea-fowl and breast fillets	Mixed with oak leaf and other fine salads for fillets	
...ith cream sauce for ...let roasts	As radicchio	With sweet–sour herb sauce for all joints	As endive and curly endive	With a strong herb sauce for all egg dishes
...s oak leaf salad	With steaks and escalopes	With herb vinaigrette as oak leaf salad	As oak leaf salad	As chicory
...ith braised meats	With roast veal, leg and steaks	With grilled poultry of all types	With stews	As chicory
...ith grapefruit for braised ...ints and boiled meats	With herb and yoghurt sauce for rolled joints	With a light herb vinaigrette for all roasted poultry	With pineapple for all roasts	With poached eggs, in a herb sauce
...ith goulash, braised meats ...d stews		With roast duck	With jugged hare and all strong stews	
...xed with cucumber for ...ulash	Mixed with cucumber for leg	With vinaigrette for turkey breast and leg		With fried eggs
	As tomatoes	As tomatoes		
	With a strong vinaigrette for all dishes	In mixed salads for all types of poultry	In mixed salads with sautées	
	Cooked as celery, raw with steaks and escalopes	Raw and cooked with roast goose and roast duck	Raw as Waldorf Salad, with all roasts	
...th sauerbraten	With breast of veal		With leg and saddle of wild boar	
...mixed salads with ...asts of all types		Only with grilled chickens		With omelettes
...be eaten raw with ...ised meats (crudités)	Mixed with apple for breast and leg			
	As celeriac	Raw and cooked to go with grilled chicken	Boiled with stews	
		With all grilled and cold poultry joints		With scrambled, fried and hard-boiled eggs
...nned, with braised ...ats		As potatoes		

INDEX OF RECIPES

English language edition © Virtue & Co., Ltd., 25 Breakfield, Coulsdon, Surrey CR3 2UE, U.K. This edition first published 1989.

Copyright © 1984/1988 by Falken-Verlag GmbH 6272 Niedernhausen., West Germany

Library of Congress Catalog Card Number 89-16527
ISBN 0-442-30277-0

Published in
the United States of America
by Van Nostrand Reinhold
115 Fifth Avenue
New York, New York 10003

Distributed in Canada
by Nelson Canada
1120 Birchmount Road
Scarborough
Ontario M1K 5G4, Canada

16 15 14 13 12 11 10 9 8 7 6 5 4 3 2 1